Herb and Lois —

Blessings on you — and

Grace and Peace!

[signature]

GOD
LOVES
THE
DANDELIONS

"I'm no rose, just a dandelion. But God must love them because He let so many of them grow and you just can't stomp them out."   (Jan Pay)

Roger Fredrikson

GOD
LOVES
THE
DANDELIONS

WORD BOOKS, PUBLISHER

WACO, TEXAS

Printed in the United States of America
Library of Congress catalog card number: 74-27481

Unless otherwise noted, all biblical quotations are from *The New English Bible,* © The Delegates of the Oxford University Press and The Syndics of the Cambridge University Press, 1961, 1970, and are reprinted by permission.

The quotation marked RSV is from The Revised Standard Version of the Bible, copyrighted 1946 (renewed 1973), 1956 and © 1971 by the Division of Christian Education of the National Council of the Churches of Christ in the U.S.A., and is used by permission.

The quotation marked Phillips is from *The New Testament in Modern English* by J. B. Phillips, © J. B. Phillips 1958, published by The Macmillan Company.

All photographs by Joel Strasser.

TO RUTH

"Power to you!"

Contents

Preface

Why does anyone write a book? I've asked myself that a dozen times during the last couple of years. Particularly when I've "run out of gas" and been all set to call it quits. But then some light has flickered or a bit of time has opened up or a word of encouragement has come. Incidentally, much of the encouragement has come from my dear friend Bruce Larson, formerly of Faith at Work.

Well, I guess you write because there's a story to tell, and you feel people ought to have a chance to hear it. Particularly if you believe it's good news!

That's what's been going on in First Baptist, Sioux Falls, South Dakota. A strong, well-organized, "regular" church in suburbia, of all places, is beginning to experience stirrings of life—deep in its innards, not just on the edges! It's beginning to open up and become a community of healing. That's good news!

It's been happening in suburban America, with a beautiful church building as a base of operations. Not in a ghetto or the inner city or some warehouse or cafe. Suburbia is where God has called us to minister. Starting with fifteen to sixteen hundred people who know all about bylaws and Robert's Rules of Order and their own tradition and really know how to say, "But we've always done it that way."

But here the Spirit is at work and new things are breaking forth. We have come to see that the Book of Acts is an open-ended book.

9

This has turned out to be an exciting pilgrimage for both people and pastor—with much joy and some pain. And we have all grown.

I am eager to thank these dear people of First Baptist who have lived with my foibles and mistakes—and my wild ideas. They have challenged me, accepted me, and loved me. Without them I could never have known the freedom of the Spirit. I love them and long to live in submission to them.

Thanks to so many of them who have allowed me to use their names in telling an unvarnished story. (This is not a "doctored" account.) They represent all the others whose names have not been mentioned, but who are nevertheless just as much a part of the story.

And thanks to our staff—patient, long-suffering and supportive. Particularly the other pastors, who are teammates in every way— Victor Balla, Byron Rogillio, and Dale Saxon.

Then there is LeeDel Howard, my faithful, understanding, but "tough" secretary. She has taken dictation by the ton, kept my schedule straight, often arranged my travel schedule—just ask the congregation about that—helped me find lost keys and papers and in general helped me keep my sanity now for more than seven years. And typed every blessed word of this book—through three or four "launderings." Where would I have been without her?

And my family. What a lovable crew—who have encouraged me beyond anything they will ever know! Not just in this writing, but in a whole style of life we have known together in Christ, which continues, even though we are separated geographically. And Ruth has been at the heart of it all—often giving up our time together and changing her plans so this writing would get done. Her gentle joy has affected everything I have tried to do now for thirty years.

If this "good news" seems disjointed and erratic here and there, it's not surprising. I have written in snatches and bits, often on the run. Between conferences and sermons, committee meetings and crisis situations, funerals and weddings without end. Much of it has been put together on planes or in motels. I notice that chapters have been completed all over the place—our summer cottage at Lobster Lake; Chautauqua, New York; the Sheraton Hotel in Dayton, Ohio; the American Baptist Assembly in Green Lake, Wisconsin; and even one chapter in Hawaii.

And, oh yes, thanks to the North American Baptist Seminary

here in Sioux Falls for the generous use of their library. And to Miller Funeral Home who furnished me with at least two dozen of their complimentary pens.

And running through it all has been the strength and grace of our Lord.

ROGER FREDRIKSON

June 1, 1974 on the eve
of fifteen years with the
Sioux Falls congregation.

1.

Standing

on

Tiptoe

We were standing in a circle at The Firehouse getting ready for another Saturday night. Like a hundred times before. And by some miracle of faithfulness and grace, a crew was on hand again to keep the place going—a businessman or two, a nurse, a couple of homemakers, a student, a teacher, a salesman, and maybe one or two others. All amateurs and volunteers, they had come to make the coffee and wash the dishes, tend the cash register, and serve the people. It would have been so much easier to spend the evening in front of a TV set. But here they were!

This night a group of young people from Kansas had joined us —the "So Loved Singers"—eager to get underway.

It was like getting ready for a party as we introduced ourselves— all that laughing and small talk. Then we reached out for one another as we tried to center down and prepare for the action. The "inner journey" we call it—a part of the discipline of ministering in The Firehouse—something we had learned from The Potter's House in Washington, D.C.

It was then that Lenora Bezpaletz voiced some simple, hushed words. Her Jim was home caring for the children so she could take her regular turn as a waitress. They came as naturally as breathing, "Lord, thanks for letting us be here tonight. We're standing on tiptoe waiting to see what you're going to do. Amen." What a way to put it—like children straining to catch a glimpse of the parade coming down the street.

Did we really expect that? Could this really be that kind of a night? Well, it was! A beautiful, noisy party!

All kinds of people came our way—the old and the young, the new and the regulars—some crashing in like they owned the place; others moving in a bit nervously hoping they'd "fit"; some squatting on the floor; and others glad to stand around the walls. The air was full of laughing and shouting, with people even joining in on the singing now and then. Here and there people made attempts at conversation, while others were content just to hold hands and take it all in. Our waiters and waitresses had quite a time squeezing around getting the coffee and pastries to the right people.

After the first "show" some people were so excited they hurried out to find their friends. These singers from Fort Scott were great. And the crowd came swinging along. On their rock version of "O Happy Day" everyone caught the beat, and The Firehouse shook and rattled.

But there were some quiet, heavy times too—particularly when Frank, the shy bass guitarist, asked if he might say something. He was the last fellow you would have expected to do a thing like that. A hush came over the room as he fumbled to find the words. Frank had met Christ that day and he simply had to let us know. Everyone stomped and cheered when he ended up by saying, "Now everything's different!"

It was almost 1:00 A.M. when we closed up shop after giving thanks for this whole wonderful night. But it wasn't over. As I started for the door a lonely, needy teenager caught me by the arm, desperate for some scrap of friendship. I ended up driving her home, listened to some of her heartache, and tried sharing a bit of hope with her.

When I finally drove into my garage, I could only sit there silently before going in, wondering about all that had taken place. Lenora's prayer—how it had been answered! We had been on tiptoe all night, catching the rhythm and beauty of God moving in our midst. He really is the "Lord of the dance."

But all that took place at a coffeehouse on a Saturday night. If God is alive and at work, then what has happened in the *church?* Where did it lose its sense of gaiety and adventure? Lose its nerve? The last place most of us expect any excitement or fire is around the church. So much of it is so proper and dull—wandering around in a maze of organization, going through motions no one understands or cares about, passing out neatly packaged programs which leave most people cold. Nothing joyous in any of this, only a slow kind of death, a hardening of the spiritual arteries. So if we had a chance to celebrate, we'd better get on with it!

All of a sudden I came to with a start. Here I was carrying on a private reverie in the wee hours. And in a short time I'd have to be back at the church for worship. So I went in, tried to turn off the excitement and get a little sleep.

But the gathering at the church building a few hours later was no letdown. It still is possible for God to show up among his people in a "regular" church service. This was the day of communion, and as we broke the bread and shared in the cup, Christ really spread his feast among us.

The So Loved Singers had stayed for the weekend. I doubt any of us will ever forget the haunting words of their song "Nobody Wanted Him" as each of us held the bread torn from the loaf and wondered about its meaning. As we lifted the cup the congregation sang "Christ the Lord Is Risen Today" with a power and freedom I have seldom heard. The Lord was dancing here too.

Then we were given some fresh, living words. Herman Van Arsdale, the pastor and beloved friend of the Singers, stood before the table and spoke of the new joy Christ had let loose in his life right in the middle of frightening need.

One of those unexpected, terrifying things we think will never happen to us had come crashing in on the Van Arsdales. Their only daughter, Debbie, an open-hearted girl who loved to make music, had gone off to church with her family some months before. Even though she had a stabbing headache, everyone assumed this would be another November Sunday. But within hours Debbie was dead—with a ruptured aneurysm. Who could have realized when she sang "O Love that wilt not let me go . . . I give Thee back the life I owe" earlier that morning that that is precisely what she would be doing before the day was finished?

Van and his wife Ruth wondered if they could ever sing again. But instead of crawling off into some hole of self-pity, the Van Arsdales let themselves get drawn into the lives of all kinds of young people in their community. Many of these were Debbie's friends. "And," as Van said, "God's hand was in all this!" So the music started to come back. Out of this friendship with the young, the So Loved Singers were drawn together. It was a simple, moving witness, full of hope.

Then Joe McAuley, of our own congregation, came to the communion table. He had taken on the failure and bitterness of a strange assortment of men at our "halfway house" over the last couple of years. While Joe shared a bit of this amazing story, his wife Edith stood at his side, her big brown eyes shining with joy.

At the invitation of our church, this brave, childlike couple had turned a huge, pink house at the edge of town into a place of hope. Men coming out of prison or alcoholic treatment—full of shakes and fear—had found a second chance because Joe and Edith and their three daughters had filled the old house with their love. No wonder it had become "The Glory House."

Joe has a refreshing, earthy way of putting things—usually creating his own language as he goes along, a little like Casey Stengel. But that day no one could miss the message. "We got no failures at the house," he said, "because we start with failures. And we're no experts. All we got to give these men is love—no fancy talk, just love! This is why we got to stay close to the 'Big Man,' so we can keep giving out that love."

Joe should know. It was love that finally saved him after twenty-three desperate years of compulsive alcoholism—love that came through the patient suffering of Edith and a few stubborn friends who refused to give up. And in the end Joe had become another story of God's incredible grace touching and healing him.

Well, it was simply a great morning! The living Lord had surprised us again—getting us up on tiptoe to see what he was about! No wonder we left rejoicing. It seemed the angels had been singing "Hallelujahs" all around us. Less noisy than The Firehouse, but just as real!

We could never have arranged or put together experiences like these in a thousand years. We're too unimaginative for that, and often far too anxious to impress one another. So we keep making simple, beautiful things—like the mystery of the moon or the story cf Jesus—into brassy, neon affairs—gilded "Superstars." But that's not the way of our Lord. His gifts come in such silent, wondrous, unexpected ways. He keeps slipping up on us through the back door. Like a host who keeps throwing magnificent parties and then invites the most unlikely characters to show up. Otherwise, how would I have been included? That's the biggest surprise of all.

How tragic that we should have lost the spirit of the party around the church. So much of it is so dismal and moralistic, even thin-lipped and grim! Is it any wonder multitudes turn to the cocktail hour and the bar? At least that's good for a few laughs and a little human companionship. And no one will be trying to straighten you out.

Take the typical trustees' meeting. "Well," you say, "they are supposed to be joyless affairs because those men are dealing with money and property matters."

All right, then, but what about worship? That's where it really ought to be! But, isn't that the same old stuff? People sitting in the same pews for decades, angered if someone takes their seat, criticizing the choice of hymns or the temperature of the building. And the preaching and the praying! How the same old phrases come forth Sunday after Sunday in the same unctuous tone of voice coming finally to the same worn-out conclusion. No sense of drama or movement in any of that. No wonder Dorothy Sayers has said that Jesus' so-called friends have done to him what his enemies would never have dreamt of doing—reduced that magnificent story, so full of mystery and power, to little trite clichés, hollow and dull![1] No wonder eager seekers turn away feeling empty and cheated and even angry. They had hoped for so much more.

But that isn't the way it was!

Yes, his life was simple and unpretentious—but all of it so unexpected. The way he came to us—the angel dealing with that slip of a girl, Mary, and the Holy Spirit brooding over her. Or the way he lived—dealing with all kinds of unsavory, offbeat characters: talking with a Samaritan woman at a well with a horrible reputation, or going to a tax collector's home for dinner. That really got the religious gossips uptight. But look what happened to that woman and that tax collector. And when his disciples were paralyzed with fear, caught in one of those vicious Galilean storms, he hushed up nature like a mother puts her child to sleep. That's the way his whole story runs. Do we really believe the days for that kind of thing are over?

And look how he died! On little more than a garbage pile between two thieves on a Roman cross. "When we were still powerless, then Christ died" for us,[2] we read. That's when God did his most incredible thing. A borrowed grave, a huge rock, a special guard, even despairing unbelief, couldn't stop the Resurrection! That's why the first Christian preacher cried out, "But God raised him to life again, setting him free from the pangs of death, because it could not be that death should keep him in its grip." [3]

Then why should the church become a dreary, boring place? We are the people of the Resurrection. Christ is alive and doing things! Why shouldn't we be running up and down the roads shouting out this good news?

And that's what I have been discovering right in the middle of the organized local church. In midwestern suburban America, no less. In the midst of endless committee meetings, hurt feelings, raising budgets, criticisms I have felt I haven't deserved, a phone that never seems to stop ringing. But most of all among enough eager, open people to make the whole thing worthwhile, and kindle in me the joy of expectation. What a place to find the Resurrection power! This has to be the greatest surprise of my life.

I am still a bit amazed that I ended up in the local church. Not because I ran out of things to do or turned to the church in desperation, but because a restless fellow like me found this to be his "home." I got into the church while I was having the time of my life working with college students as a chaplain and instructor at my alma mater, Ottawa University in Ottawa, Kansas. I suppose I could have stayed at that for another dozen years. These students had been my meat and drink for five years. I had come there right out of seminary, freshly ordained, with a Master of Sacred Theology, certain I was ready for anything. Well, not quite!

Because, among other things, that back row of worldly wise veterans just home from the Korean War almost took care of me. My seminary notes and that new diploma didn't seem to impress them too much. Their hard-hitting, unvarnished questions in that 10:00 section of Religion 105 often sent me home licking my wounds wondering if I could ever face them again.

Or there were those tenderly sarcastic freshmen who dubbed my introductory course "Remedial Religion." And there were a host of beautiful friendships among the students and faculty. I couldn't walk away from all this and a lot more without some serious second thoughts.

There were friends who insisted I must have lost my marbles—leaving all that excitement with students for the graveyard known as the local church. Why, anyone who was on the "in" knew the institutional church was on its last legs. And the sooner we had a respectable funeral the better.

But how was I to deal with an inner restlessness that simply wouldn't let me go? Something in me longed to take on a church, and I simply couldn't shake it. Finally I became convinced this must be the calling of God. At least I had to give it a try. This is the only way I can explain jumping into the church. Perhaps it is more correct to say I was "chosen."

I ended up becoming the pastor of the very church to which I belonged—half a mile from the college. And what seems even odder, I was a member of the committee looking for a new pastor. Friends asked for weeks afterwards, "How did you manage to arrange that?" Well, it was a move full of unusual twists to say the least, none of them contrived as far as I know. The First Baptist Church of Ottawa, Kansas, was full of great old tradition, and its life was woven into the fabric of the community in an unusual way. The story of the Ottawa Indians and John Tecumseh Jones is all a part of the history of that area.

My first sermon was preached on a cold, raw Sunday early in February of 1954. I was weak and empty, not only because I was nervous about this new beginning, but because we had just returned from my father's funeral. Amid the snow and pine trees of Evergreen Cemetery in central Minnesota we had put Dad to rest on Monday of that week. So I came to the pulpit emotionally drained, full of long, intimate memories.

Dad was a man of refreshing, earthy humor, completely at home among the farming people whom he served for thirty-five years through a series of country pastorates. There was a kind of joyful abandon about whatever he did—whether it was the struggle to keep the church furnace in repair, or hauling those endless pails of water to get the baptistry full in time for the big event, or yanking me back in line after another of those scrapes I seemed to be constantly getting into, or sharing the Message which was the passion of his life—always best in his native Swedish.

He held nothing back. Even in his last struggle with cancer he fought it to the end. In spite of all the disappointments and always little or no money—Mother and I borrowed the money for his funeral expenses because he died inches away from poverty—Dad never lost his simple, radiant faith!

My mind was full of all this as I stood to preach that first sermon. I launched forth by asking, "Is the church a live option?" and tried to muster as strong an answer as possible. After all, hadn't our Lord said he would build a community that even hell couldn't overthrow? But most of all I spoke about what I had seen and known in my father's life. It seemed to be the best evidence at hand for the tough, undying nature of God's people.

That was the beginning—my first faltering step into the give-and-take of parish life, the beginning of my education. Much of it loving and warm and supportive, but some of it disillusioning and disheartening.

I recall going home from my first trustees' meeting with a nervous, let-down feeling, almost sick to my stomach. Was this negative, critical attitude, even toward paying our monthly bills, going to determine our outreach as a church? And it was a shocker to run into the critical, judgmental attitudes some of the members had toward others in the same church family. Many of these went back years to old slights and hurt feelings. Or there was that deadly response, "But we've never done it that way before." How was I to handle that? But it was my congregation and this was part of my growing up.

And they had to live with me too. Every now and then my hot Swedish temper would get out of hand and I'd blow up. I'd usually make some nasty, unkind statement that I'd have to go and straighten out later if I was going to live with myself. Or there was that subtle temptation to make things look better so I could get my own way in a certain matter. And often I'd get terribly pushy and messianic in my preaching. I was going to save the world with sermons. But, wonder of wonders, the people accepted me and loved me and allowed me to go ahead.

Early in my ministry in that place, I began to feel more and more that the traditional "eight to five, preacher-centered, two services on Sunday and a Wednesday night prayer meeting" would never make it in the hectic, uncertain postwar years. I certainly didn't have the answers. So I began to reach out and snoop around, hoping to learn from other ministers and churches—wherever reality seemed to be breaking forth. I visited The Church of The Saviour in Washington, D.C., got to one of Elton Trueblood's Yokefellow Conferences where I met Sam Shoemaker and Bob Raines and some beautiful lay people. I even stumbled into Alcoholics Anonymous quite by accident.

And what I had suspected all along was true. There were all kinds of believing, expectant people around, who were convinced that the best days for the living church were just ahead. And God was using them to bring forth many differing styles of authentic ministry. This could really be an age of hope—in spite of the doom peddlers.

Apparently some of the excitement I found in these places began to leak through in my day-to-day ministry. Because a word of affirmation concerning this came from a completely unexpected source. Mrs. Otto Wolgast—Mae as I came to call her even though she was in her mid-seventies then—was one of our solid citizens. Through the years she had taken on all the regular church assignments—women's society, Sunday school, deaconess, and all the rest. She was somehow aware of my restless seeking and one day whispered at the door, "Keep right on, pastor. I'm with you all the way." She only grinned as I stared back in wonderment. Here was one of the living people, right in the middle of the establishment, who knew more about God's new age than I ever could have imagined.

And over the years enough of that kind of people have always seemed to show up at the right time.

Early in those Ottawa years I met Joe McAuley, and he opened up for me the world of the alcoholic, with its despair and failure and wasted years. But also with the desperate hope for something better. Through Joe I came to know his friends. What a collection! It was like going to school all over again. Talk about intriguing escapades. Like the night we took Finnell Ward to an A.A. treatment center in Kansas City, and all the way up we nursed him along with his Old Crow so he wouldn't slip off into d.t.'s. Nothing in seminary had prepared me for that.

Or there was the time word came that Abe Lantz—a strong, angry man, a "cat skinner" for a construction company—was out to get me, gun in hand. He had gotten miffed over some little misunderstanding—not unusual for alcoholics, or some of the rest of us—and friends called to warn me. Not long afterwards Abe ended it all. He drove his car out into a ravine and left the motor running with the exhaust piped into the car. Seven days later the sheriff found him, badly discolored, slumped over the wheel. With a paperback turned toward the window, cover page up, I WANT TO LIVE. A cry for help too late. We tried our best to put together some kind of a helpful funeral service for his family.

It was heartwarming to see the way the church people rejoiced in this new involvement. When some of these noisy, obvious sinners began to show up at our services they were welcomed as friends. Their zest and an earthy realism helped keep the rest of us honest. As one of our deacons put it, "Maybe the Lord is sending these people to us." We couldn't argue with that.

Then one day there was a call from the jail. (Nothing like traveling in top-flight company!) A fellow named Paul Edwards had been picked up coming into town after smashing headlong into a bridge abutment. He was trying to get home to Wichita after a week-long drinking spree, utterly convinced someone was chasing him. The state highway patrol came along shortly and picked him up.

Paul had ducked out on a Boy Scout Blue and Gold Banquet, his job, and all his responsibilities. He had failed his son and everyone else, so what could he do but take off with his bottle—an old alcoholic trick. And here he sat in the Ottawa jail, sick and scared.

The fine was $126, with thirty days in jail which would be suspended for good behavior. And, bless them, our deacons were willing to pick up the tab for the fine out of the "fellowship fund" —a new kind of risk for all of us. But one of the Wichita A.A. people, Al Hendricks, strongly urged us by phone to let Paul face the music and pay his own fine. "Otherwise, he'll never grow up," he said. So Paul sold what was left of the car for salvage, paid the fine, and left for home with his wife and brother-in-law. But not before we had broken bread together at a truckers' stop at the edge of town. And this the deacons paid for.

Years later Paul wrote me: "I knelt down on the floor of that lousy jail and prayed for help. (You had been there the night before.) I didn't think it was much of a prayer at the time, but maybe it was the most effective prayer of my life. Anyway, since then, I have had over seventeen and one-half years of blessed

I'm still amazed
that I ended up
in the local church.

It is God's gift which frees the pastor to share a
chunk of his life with a group of men at breakfast.

sobriety." And every year the Edwards send us a Christmas card with a note of thanks.

Talk about a miracle! And I had been privileged to be in on it. But it wasn't just alcoholics. It was far more than that. I had really been wanting to get to know some of our men, not to promote anything—stewardship or prayer or church attendance—but just as brothers in Christ. So I threw out an invitation and about a dozen of them showed up for a time of sharing and prayer. We met at 6:45 on a Tuesday morning in the church kitchen—a beautiful cross section of everything we had in the church. Willa Henderson, one of those joyous, free spirits, asked if she might not get the eggs and bacon ready for our gathering. I doubt if any early morning men's group has ever eaten any better.

The gathering was like a party. After the first, almost embarrassed, testing of the experience, the men began to buy in with one another. They were surprised by the spirit of trust and openness and love that began to carry the group along. The questions and affirmations and prayers began to pour forth freely. We really became a band of brothers. And they gave me more than I could ever share with them. I have never lived without some kind of group like that since that day.

And so I began to stumble into more and more excitement right in the middle of the establishment. Like the visit of Betty O'Connor and Paul Coggins from The Church of The Saviour and Paul and Eleanor Offill from Calvary Episcopal Church in Pittsburgh coming to share with our people. What a time we had, long before I knew anything about Faith at Work!

Then a couple of small groups got going, one on Wednesday mornings for women and another for couples on Sunday nights. It was almost more than I could handle at times. More and more I found a rising tide of expectancy within me and among those with whom I ministered.

Now this did not come to pass because our church had a "good" reputation or because I was fortunate in having an excellent professional theological training or by getting into a building program as we did. No, actually all this could have kept me from "standing on tiptoe." "How hard it will be for the wealthy to enter the kingdom of God!" [4] No, childlike wonder and trust are a gift—a gift of the Spirit. And there is no cut and dried formula for accepting this gift—only the willingness and humility to receive. Here we are dealing with surrender and trust, repentance and obedience. And that happens only in the hidden, deeply intimate part of myself. Here is where we struggle to let go, so the old can die and the new be born. This is embarrassing business—because I'd really like to be self-sufficient. Who wants to go to the bloody cross to accept this kind of death? But that is the only way the Spirit can bring us into the power of the Resurrection, no longer under condemnation—with nothing to prove and no false guilts to lug around. Now I'm really "free to be me" in Christ, and that's where the joy and spontaneity are!

This process can be awfully specific and painful. It touches me right where I'd like to be strong and in charge of things. Like today—right in the middle of writing this chapter. Ruth and I are here at our small cabin at Lobster Lake, our small, primitive retreat place up by Alexandria, Minnesota. We have just finished reading some beautiful words from the Epistle to the Philippians for our morning worship: "My God will supply all your wants." . . . "I have strength for anything through him who gives me power." . . . "The peace of God, which is beyond our utmost understanding, will keep guard over your hearts and your thoughts, in Christ Jesus." [5] Then a time of open, free prayer.

And now breakfast. So I crack open my boiled egg, and it comes out watery and partially raw. Irritating, because I have a built-in prejudice against half-boiled eggs. I can't understand why anyone, even Ruth, can't watch the time more carefully when it comes to boiling eggs.

But I try to brush it all aside as if it doesn't matter, all the time trying to scoop up the stringy egg—peeved, and then angered with myself that I am letting an egg frustrate me. So we finish breakfast in a rather tense silence.

Then I go off to write about new life and hope in the church, assuming that people are eagerly waiting for some scrap of encouragement or word of wisdom from the great one! But an unboiled egg has thrown me.

All of a sudden the pettiness and shame of it all hits me. And by some minor miracle I am able to turn and walk back up to the cabin, at first all uncomfortable, but finally able to blurt out, "Ruth, you know how the egg got me. I just can't understand myself.

Here we've read these beautiful promises and it's a glorious day and we're together—and I'm hung up on an egg. Will you forgive me?" And then we have a good laugh about it.

I must confess that the nudge which moved me from frustration to cleansing laughter is a gift, God's gift. And now the whole day is changed. All kinds of new possibilities have opened up.

It is this same gift which frees the pastor—hands all sweaty, certain he's now going to lose his religious authority, whatever that is—to share quietly a chunk of his life with a group of men at a breakfast. "Fellows, I'm scared and lonely and I need you." And that gift of grace can even bring a hardened old Baptist to ask with tears, "Is that you talking to me, Lord? Because if it is, then I've got to go do it." That is where the miracle starts! And it's what gets us up on our tiptoes!

2.
Signs
of His
Presence

And then we moved. On the surface it was the wrong thing to do—especially the timing. After all, we were just getting into the swing of things in Ottawa. But deep down I knew it was the only thing I could do. Had I known how painful it was all going to be, I wonder if we would have made the move.

How do you leave people who have loved and nourished you through the years? Like Ben and Jean Park, who had spent the night drinking coffee with us after my brother Gerry was killed in one of those freak car accidents late one Sunday afternoon. A college senior just starting to find himself. Or Ed and Ethiel Haley, who were game for all kinds of new and untried ventures—leading out in a building program, or entertaining Gert Behanna just after her *The Late Liz* [1] had been published. Or Andrew Martin, the president of Ottawa University, a friend and confidant, more a brother than my superior. Our golfing matches were fearsome affairs, but the conversation and camaraderie were something else. And his wife Marjorie had been such a great friend to Ruth.

And our children. How could we ask them to pull up stakes and move to another place? Ottawa had been the only life they had known.

I'm not certain this kind of thing can be logically explained. All I know is another congregation got hold of me, and I couldn't shake it. There was no way I could dismiss their quietly insistent invitation. It had to do with something far deeper than salary arrangements or the size of the congregation or the appeal of the community. Somehow I felt God was in it, my name was on it, and that left me no argument. Like a fire from which I could turn only at the risk of losing something very precious.

What began as a casual telephone visit with those persistent people in Sioux Falls, South Dakota—"How can you be certain you're supposed to stay where you are unless you come up and take a look at us?" Norm Wilson had said—got under my skin, and I finally ended up paying them a visit. That got me into the struggle, and then we had to decide.

We had a lovely dinner together—this pulpit committee and I—when I finally got up there. They were a great group of people, and we had an evening full of exciting talk. Right in the middle of it, a gifted, concerned woman, Janet DeWitt, voiced a kind of wistful comment that drew me up short. She said it softly. "Well, you know, we really are a spiritually hungry church." I wonder if she realized then what she was saying. Because I guess I knew at that moment what we would end up doing.

Some months later we went through all those tear-stained goodbyes. None of them was any more touching than the farewell party given by the A.A. Club. It was a night full of great stories, much laughter, and a few tears. Every shining face in that room was a miracle. And at the end I was given an honorary membership in the Ottawa club signed by Arloe Halbach, the secretary, who later died of tuberculosis in Colorado. Sober! Every time I open my billfold now I'm reminded of God's grace!

I shall never forget that hot June day fifteen years ago when we drove into "our" new community. Of course, I had to take the family by our new church home, a great Georgian colonial building with a clean-cut steeple pointing high above the neighborhood. But our three children weren't too impressed. Their hearts were back in Kansas. What is any building compared with friends left behind? They really seemed much more taken with all the beer joints and saloons on North Main which gave them the feeling this might be quite a frontier town. But Randy, our oldest, then in the "model building" stage, came alive a little when we discovered a couple of shops handling all kinds of models.

Now Sioux Falls is not the jumping-off place at the end of the world some people imagine it to be. Every once in a while I catch that peculiar tone when someone asks, "Let's see now, you're still in Sioux Falls, aren't you?" And I can almost catch that feeling— "Poor guy!"

But it isn't that way at all! We found Sioux Falls a community stirring with all kinds of life. Not just because of all the lovely homes surrounded by beautiful elm and ash trees, so many of them with well-manicured lawns—we noticed that right away. But it was all the sharp, eager people we began to meet. Many of them had rolled up their sleeves and launched out on some kind of a venture—business or community or cultural or what-have-you—with little more than a dream and a nickel and a lot of faith. And that seemed to give the place a fresh kind of excitement.

That first summer we picnicked here and there in the lovely parks, and our children were really delighted that they could swim in either of the two huge municipal swimming pools free. We even got to a couple of outdoor band concerts at McKennan Park and honked our car horn with everyone else to show our appreciation. I thought that tradition had died long ago, but not here.

We heard about the Southeastern Mental Health Clinic and Family Service and the South Dakota Children's Home—all home-grown projects. I visited the remarkable Crippled Children's School and Morrell's meat packing plant—Sioux Falls's largest single industry with about three thousand employees—and was utterly enthralled by it all. As they say, "We use everything but the squeal." And I believe it—with the hog pancreas being used for insulin, the pituitary gland for ACTH, and the leftovers for fertilizers. In my hospital calling I discovered that people were coming here from all around for medical help. And our children really seemed to enjoy their school experience when they got underway in the fall.

Until the first Edison Junior High social when Randy came home early and went stalking upstairs without saying a word. This seemed strange, because he had gotten ready for it so carefully— hair, clothes, and all. When I finally went up to find out the problem, he really hit me with his angry disappointment. "Why did we ever leave Ottawa and come to this awful town? I haven't got a single friend. Everybody got asked to someone's home except me!" I stood there helpless, sharing his misery more than he ever realized, wondering if we had really done right after all in moving to Sioux Falls. Is there anything worse than that awful feeling of not belonging? A score of my own painful childhood parsonage memories came crowding in—all those times when I had been left standing outside, pressing my nose against some window longing to get in, with no one seeming to care. I tried to comfort him that night, and was comforted myself to see that he kept going and eventually made it in great style.

Lots of other things have happened since we arrived—a new Interstate highway system surrounding us, a beautifully efficient air terminal, and a sports arena. Here an all-Russian basketball team played a championship American team before the largest crowd on their whole American tour, which included Madison Square Garden and Denver and a few other places. And that in the middle of the cold war. Then there is the very unusual Great Plains Zoo, and the training center for the physically and mentally handicapped, a senior citizens' center, urban renewal going on all over the place—and at least a dozen new church buildings. I'm not trying to play Chamber of Commerce—just wanted you to have a feel of what we had gotten into!

But there are other things that we don't talk about as much. Our state penitentiary with its high Indian population, the Norton-Froehlich addition which for years has been a kind of no man's land of substandard housing. Or any Indian living here can tell you about how he broke in—if he did—getting a job, finding a house, and the rest, in spite of the obstacles and apathy. Or the unusually high number of alcoholics—one treatment center in Minneapolis speaks of Sioux Falls as "Sin City" because of the large number of our people coming there for treatment. And we've been wrestling with the tough problem of drug abuse like everyone else. A friend who recently was a nondrinking guest at a cocktail party reported spontaneously, "Well, on the basis of what I heard in a couple of hours, this town really has its own Peyton Place."

In the southwestern section of this city, right next to Jefferson School at 22nd and Covell, stands First Baptist. Two blocks from Sioux Valley Hospital and three blocks from Sioux Falls College, surrounded by a great residential area. With little more than an audacious faith and a lifting spirit of sacrifice—really what else do you need—this congregation made the move from downtown in 1951 when that area was little more than a hayfield. An aggressive ministry under a courageous, creative pastor, August M. Hintz, had reached out to touch the whole community and really packed them in. And the old building at 8th and Spring simply could not hold either the people or the excitement.

The land for the new church came as a gift, completely unexpected, from Winifred Jones, whose whole life was an unselfish gift to the church. And that was the story of this congregation— living by faith and God's surprises!

It was Grandma Cummins, a stubborn, believing shut-in, who literally prayed First Baptist into existence. For ten years she waited and yearned for God to bring a family of believers together here in this frontier town of five hundred souls. Three failures during those years—the horse and buggy got swamped in the creek coming from Dell Rapids once, then someone forgot the key for Allens Hall where the gathering was to be held another time, and apparently the preacher forgot to show up the last time— failed to daunt this Baptist sister's spirit. She only "laid hold on God all the harder." On July 4, 1875—of all days—a small group of thirteen believers got themselves organized into a congregation in the home of A. W. Hauser. The faith of Grandma Cummins had finally borne fruit.

So this is where our ministry got underway. Our first Sunday was like the beginning of a marriage, or perhaps better the start of a romance that might lead to marriage. Pastor and people meeting and sizing each other up. I will always remember their hearty, friendly laugh when I spoke of the "minister having to comfort the afflicted and afflict the comfortable." This may have had a special meaning in the air-conditioned sanctuary where we were worshiping.

We were eager to meet people like John and Olive Cressey who had written us a tender, personal note of welcome. These were very special folks still carrying on a love affair after about fifty years together, younger in spirit than most teenagers, and interested in everything going on! John had been a part of almost everything the community had tackled since the year one. And there was Bob Lewis, chairman of the committee which had gotten us into all this. They were the ones who were really stuck with us.

Well, it was a great beginning. I threw myself into everything from preaching to calling with such a verve and gusto that I'm certain some of the people must have been overwhelmed. Wonderful crowds showed up almost every time we opened the doors. I even got through my first wedding in good style.

But as we went on—week after week—with all that good feeling, I began to wonder about that spiritual "nerve." Where was it? Everyone appeared so self-sufficient and hard-working. The church seemed to have everything going for it—air conditioning and a hefty parking lot; the "achievement award" for a topnotch Sunday school; a tremendous reputation for accomplishment; and gifted, capable people all over the place.

Then what had I come here to do? At times I felt very much on the outside—a glorified chaplain standing at the edge of real life, nice to have around, but really how necessary? Keeping the organization going, or praying reasonably well at public functions now and then wasn't my idea of getting at the big issues. These were being settled, it seemed, at places like the Elks Club or in the Grill Room at Minnehaha, at the bridge foursome, or the plain old neighborhood coffee. Then I began to wonder if I had made some kind of a colossal blunder coming to this place. That really began to tie me up in knots.

I had come here assuming I would be the bearer of some kind of renewal, fresh from victories elsewhere. But who was interested in that sort of thing? The temperature in the sanctuary or the double fortissimo of the organ prelude seemed more important to many of the people. So when business went on as usual, I found myself becoming more and more frustrated. And God, who must have a wonderful sense of humor, let me wallow in my own self-pity.

Certainly part of this lost, uncertain feeling was a nostalgia for the fresh excitement that was breaking forth in the Ottawa church when we had left. I guess I was just plain homesick.

And surely part of it was my own impatient, restless make-up. We had been here only a few weeks when I was asking, "Why doesn't something start happening?" And I was hanging a lot of that on my own ability to deliver.

But when I told myself all this, I knew there was something deeper. It had to do with the struggle of the church to find its own soul and mission in this "new age." Not only in the inner city

We found Sioux Falls a community stirring with all kinds of life. And since we arrived lots of other things have happened—a new Interstate system for one.

which had been getting all the publicity, but in suburbia. Here the battle lines were not open and jagged as in the ghetto. They were more hidden and genteel, but just as dirty and tough! Here it was the cultural assumption that church ought to be a part of everyone's life. "Otherwise, where do you go to get married or buried?" But what difference does that make? Then why belong?

It was like asking the fierce, embarrassing question that was the thrust of Sören Kierkegaard's whole life. "How can a Christian be a Christian?" And, as he put it, the tragedy was that the wild geese, who once had known how to freely fly the open sky, had sold out for the security of the farmer's yard. They had become so fat and domesticated they could no longer fly.

Here in suburbia the church can easily become merely one other item in the midst of everything else. "I have so many other things to get done. I must get Johnnie and Susan to their swimming lessons and the little league baseball game, or to their dancing lesson, or their cheerleading practice, or their riding lesson, or whatever other lessons there are. And I have a golf match, and then there is my bridge foursome, and there's tennis, and then the neighborhood coffee. And Pete will be getting home on Friday and I know he'll want a cookout with the Swansons. Saturday we must get the lawn taken care of, and when else can we get out for a little fun except Saturday night? And, oh yes, there is Sunday. . ." And that's where it gets tacked on.

None of this is really bad. Much of it is good. But where is the rhyme and reason of it all? The ceaseless round week after week, month after month—and finally a lifetime has been spent. And what has been the end of it all? Have there been any priorities? How much of all this is "plastic" and unreal?

So the church becomes one other activity in that round of busyness, a caboose at the end of a train. And we have to ask if the church is simply around to get into the competition and hope it can pick up a "fair share" of the time and energy of its members. What sense can "Jesus Christ is Lord" or the "people of God" make in this kind of world? Sounds a little quaint, doesn't it?

Part of this becomes the game of keeping up with everyone else. Subtle, but deadly! The salaries, the promotion, the clothes, the names we drop, who got invited to which party, who has built the latest house and where, what clubs we're in, and what deals we make— Listen to it! Feel it! That awful anxiety running through so much of it, the fear that I may be left out.

How does anyone get off that merry-go-round to become simply himself? Do the things he wants to do? Set his own pace of life? Read some of the books he's always promised himself he was going to look into? Or simply play with the children once again? How can he do that? It's a nervous, unspoken cry felt in so many places.

Now this is not meant to be a caricature, nor a cheap, easy put-down of a part of the world I have come to love. It is meant to be a sharing of the confusion I felt, a portrayal of the spirit of this suburban world I had entered, the ethos, the air it breathes. And this was where I was supposed to minister. But how? Where could I start? Did anyone really want to be a "transformer" instead of a "conformer"? A "world changer" rather than being squeezed into its mold to use the words of J. B. Phillips? [2] If so, how could they be called forth?

Well, that was an order far too vast for me. Certainly my easy-going, gregarious, friendly way with people, a kind of turned-on charm for Jesus, would never be equal to this task.

So more and more a feeling of self-pity and helplessness seemed to engulf me. Like Moses crying out to God when the call was laid on him, "But who am I . . . that I should go to Pharaoh, and that I should bring the Israelites out of Egypt?" [3] And all the time I was "playing church," wondering how I could get out of it.

But I was saved by an unexpected gift—something I would never have planned, because it was too simple. And it slipped in quietly through the back door. Almost unannounced.

It started at our national church convention some months earlier in Des Moines. A dozen or so fellows had gotten together for an evening of talk—mostly about the church. How could a new thing come? Little by little our fears and angers and longings came leaking out—a strange mixture of frustration and hope. And the more honest we became the more our defenses came tumbling down, until finally we discovered one another, not as professional competitors, but as a band of brothers reaching out for one another. At least, we agreed, we could keep in touch and pray for one another. And we certainly needed that. We even set a time— "as near six in the morning as possible."

Well, as beautiful as the evening had been, I remember thinking at the time, "It's really the same old stuff. You get a bunch of preachers together and they always end up agreeing to pray for one another." There is nothing quite like the hardness of a religious pro's heart.

But in spite of it, I determined to keep my end of the bargain when I got home, even though much of the time I didn't feel like it. So every morning at about six I would crawl stubbornly out of bed, splash some cold water on my face, throw on some clothes, walk down to the church five blocks away, and get on my knees in the chapel or my study. And try to pray. But it was a barren wilderness with no joy or lift in it. And no sign of a Presence! A futile exercise—going through motions which had no meaning.

But every time I was about to give up or get out I would hear from one of the other fellows. A note or a phone call—just wondering how I was getting along. These fellows were really taking this prayer thing far more seriously than I had dared imagine. There was no way I could drop out without giving some kind of honest explanation to the others, and this I couldn't bring myself to do. So I hung on for dear life.

Then one day there came a stirring. Not much, but enough. Just a small breath of life. How can I explain it? Do I need to? How had that opening come, however small, so there could be a new beginning? Was it that band of stubborn, beautiful ministers lifting up my name every day? Were there people right here in Sioux Falls unknown to me who somehow realized what was going on and "remembered me"? Was it the desperate bottom I had hit which left me with no "out"—least of all my own strength or ingenuity—except that great, merciful God who loved me? In spite of everything.

I do not know. But he had dealt with me in his own way, mysterious and painful as that might be, and now the quiet power of his Holy Spirit began to flood my life. I was overwhelmed with gratitude—joyful and inexpressible. He had not left me!

I wish I could say that was the last time I got into that kind of a spiritual jam. But it isn't. I have had to learn again and again that I cannot play "big man" for God—however much I may push or manipulate or convince myself that this particular plan is the will of God. I can only thank him for his patience with me.

And this congregation. How could I be so blind? These people had been given to me as my particular joy and burden. And just because I couldn't pull off something big in the first few months did not mean he didn't have a very special plan for them—for us. After all, he had loved these people long before I'd come along.

So my eyes were opened. And that spirit of expectancy began to fill my life once again. That's when my real ministry got under-way. For his sake, not for mine. Far more unpretentious than I had planned—now and then a nudge or a hint being dropped here or there, almost imperceptible. Like doors being quietly opened which I was invited to enter. And unmistakable signs of his presence in the congregation.

First it was Bob Olson. I had heard about him. He had some strong opinions about the way things ought to be going around the church. Al Babcock, our really great minister of Christian Education at the time, had said, "You'll have to meet Bob Olson." Bob had come from Chicago to attend Sioux Falls College and had liked the community, the people—and the hunting. And it was Anna's home state. So after medical training at the University of Illinois he had returned to begin his practice.

Well, I was mowing the lawn one Saturday evening, trying to get it done before Sunday—a little like the old Saturday night bath —when Bob pulled up in his Thunderbird. Of course, I was happy to stop the mower, and he threw out some remark about "a preacher trying to mow his own lawn." That got us into some good-natured banter about this and that and the good old days.

Finally we got around to the church, and then we went in for a cup of coffee. Deep down Bob was disturbed by the church—not hostile, but disappointed. He felt it had let him down. He was looking for so much more than he was getting. When he had tried to serve as a deacon some years before, it had been a frustrating experience. "Too much mickey mouse," was the way he put it. I discovered that night Bob would never keep you in the dark about what he was thinking.

When he had been approached about a gift for the new educational building, the size of the request had embarrassed him. As he bluntly said, "Why, that kind of a pledge wouldn't have re-quired any faith. I don't know why they even bothered to ask me."

Imagine! This man had stopped by on his own to let me in on all this. Had he not cared he never would have come! And what

I heard him saying was, "I am available, but I want the church to stop playing games." I wonder if Bob even guessed what a gift his visit turned out to be! It was the beginning of a warm, and I must say challenging, friendship.

When I finally put the mower away I hardly realized it was dark or that I hadn't finished the lawn. Too much excitement had been kicked up for that kind of concern. Who would have thought that on a Saturday night there would have been this kind of a knock on the door and I would begin to discover the face of my parish? I could not help wondering, "How many other seeking, wistful 'Bobs' are there in this congregation who are simply waiting?" When I finally turned in for the night I remember thinking, "Brother, I'm going to find a place for you if it's the last thing I do."

Not long afterwards it was Peggy. I knew her only casually—a lovely, chic housewife I had seen around the church. Certainly she had everything most people want—a beautiful home and a very attractive family, all kinds of friends and a constant round of activities. What else could you ask for? Peggy had been in the church all her life, usually helping out whenever the call came.

But when she came to the office that day it was not to pass the time of day on pleasantries. She came right to the point. She was sick unto death of all those surface friendships and running around in circles. None of it had filled the aching void at the center of her life. She yearned for reality. And all those things she had done in the church had not brought peace or deliverance. It was all said so deliberately and thoughtfully that I could tell she had been wanting to dump it out somewhere for a long time. And it came so directly it took my breath away. Then I noticed the tears trickling quietly down her face.

We sat there hushed for a few moments, certain that another Presence had joined us and was brooding over this whole affair. So much like all those beautiful encounters in the Gospels— Nicodemus at night, the woman at the well, Zacchaeus in his home, and now here in the suburban church.

That day Peggy reached out and very quietly gave herself to Christ—a breathless, trembling act of faith. Her prayer was a cry, like a child coming home. And what a welcome the Father gave her! With a feast and all the trimmings. Even I could hear music and dancing.

And this was no temporary, emotional jag. So often we hear that accusation. Peggy was born anew, an act of the Spirit that doesn't peter out. A quiet radiance began to fill her life, and everything was touched by it—her family, the people in the neighborhood, her P.T.A. responsibility, her country club friends, and all the rest! You can't hide good news like that! It leaks out in a hundred ways. To this day she is Christ's woman. Another sign of God's presence!

After Peggy had gone I simply sat there, grateful, knowing that these really were "my" people! I, too, was coming home. This really was where God wanted me. And I would stay until he told me to go elsewhere.

3.

The
Open
Agenda

Not long after this we took a risk. We decided to open our church, not just from 8:00 to 5:00, but twenty-four hours a day. And we have never been the same.

That decision sneaked up on us. It started in our board of trustees of all places. One of our church school teachers needed a key to get in after hours. How else could she prepare her room for Sunday when she worked all week and we locked up at five? Strange how difficult we can make it for the faithful ones.

That's how this item got on the trustees' agenda. After all, they're responsible for the building. "Well," one of the men said when the matter came up, "certainly we'll have to get her a key. But what about the other teachers? Maybe we ought to find out how many we need altogether."

Then one of the other men blurted out a completely unexpected suggestion. "Why not simply open up the whole building? That would take care of the key business. And there might even be some people who would like to come in and pray after hours." There was a little nervous laughter on that, before all kinds of strenuous objections came tumbling out. "How in the world can we ever consider opening our million-dollar building for any Tom, Dick, or Harry?" "Don't we know there are all kinds of vandals and wild-eyed people just waiting for that kind of a chance? They'll tear the place up in no time." "And certainly our insurance people will never hear of such a foolhardy venture." The clincher seemed to be, "If there aren't any other churches staying open, then why should we?"

So the matter was closed—we thought! We'd have a few more keys made up for the teachers who really needed them.

But at the next monthly trustees' meeting this business of the church being open came up again. I no longer recall who was "foolish" enough to mention it, but it certainly wasn't an item on the agenda. So once again, after a brief, opinionated discussion, the matter was dropped.

But we were stuck with an issue, and couldn't seem to get it off our backs. Because at the next meeting here it came again. Certainly not due to any of my arranging. As a matter of fact, by this time I had become an intensely fascinated observer, wondering how it was all going to come out.

By now we had gotten beyond the question of property values or the protection of our building. These men were asking, "What is right?" Of course, they had a responsibility for this property. But what about people in the building at night? Was that their business? It was a completely absorbing discussion—these professional men asking themselves what it meant to be faithful Christian stewards of both property and a ministry. Then they got to the heart of the matter. "How much are we supposed to be open to people?" And that's where the issue was decided.

It was Walt Bones, a farmer and cattle feeder, who helped settle it. He told us how he had attended an Episcopal church in St. Paul as a boy. And, as he remembered it, this church stood open all the time. "Isn't a church building supposed to be a sanctuary?" he asked. "Well, that may mean one thing to a church crowd, but I know what it means to a hunter—and you all know how I feel about hunting. A sanctuary is a place where wild game can't be touched. It's a refuge. Not even I can shoot anything there. Maybe this is what our church building ought to be—a hideout, a safe place where anyone can come who needs help and no one can get at him. If that's right, then I believe we ought to open up."

That word carried the day. It was unanimously agreed we would open the church for three months and see what happened. The main outside doors would stand open all the time with only a few critical areas inside the church—like the kitchen and boiler room and offices—locked during the night. I was surprised how quickly our insurance people approved of this.

It was a faltering, tentative decision, but an act of faith. And that's what counts. We were sticking our necks out a little, saying, "Here we are, available in a new way." And we have never been able to turn back.

I shall always remember that first "open night." Some of us stood by the main doors in the early evening and gave the whole building once again to the Lord. As I drove away I noticed the warm glow—like an invitation—coming from the light at the front of the chapel. We had agreed to leave a couple of lights on up at the front.

That invitation was quickly accepted. Within a month two needy people came our way reaching out for help—like signs from our Lord, confirming what we had done. And both discovered that the church can be a sanctuary.

The first was a sixteen-year-old boy who had run away from home. He came stumbling into our church one night, desperate and ill. The light was shining in one of the third-story windows, and he had come in hoping to find a friend. Well, it was a Sunday school teacher who was up in that room, getting things ready for the coming Sunday. Quite appropriate! When she heard noises, she hurried down to check and found this trembling, feverish boy. Then she called our home, and I hurried down.

But he was not about to spill out his troubles to a minister, regardless of how miserable he felt. I smacked too much of some kind of official authority.

So I called Bob Olson for some help, and he was the answer. After he checked the boy's temperature and gave him a good dose of antibiotics, out came the story. He had gotten disgusted with things at home like most fellows his age do sooner or later. That's when he struck out on a lark, heading for the bright lights of Sioux Falls, seventy miles to the east. But it didn't turn out to be all that great. After one night on a park bench and the second on the ground trying to keep warm with newspapers and maps, walking the streets during the day, with no friends and hardly any money, he was lonely and scared and on the verge of pneumonia. That's when he showed up at the church—eager for some kind of friendship.

So we took him back to his home—Bob and I. Hardly speaking a word the whole way. It was almost as if we were both thinking this could have been one of our boys. But as we neared Mitchell our friend in the back seat got more and more excited, and almost stumbled out before we could get the car stopped at the all-night truckers' stop where his mother worked. And to watch that mother welcome her son home, warmly and unashamedly, in the middle of customers and coffee orders, was something simply unforgettable.

For a few moments it seemed the church had been in the middle of life. On the way home, after a cup of coffee, Bob and I talked about that. Maybe this open door business was going to turn out to be more than any of us realized.

And that was exactly right. A few nights later I crawled out of bed to answer the shrill ringing of the phone. No sound like it! And always so difficult to find the little monster at that time of the night. Why does it always ring at 2:00 A.M.? I was greeted by a thick, inebriated voice at the other end of the line—unfamiliar at first, and then I remembered. A few months earlier I had officiated at his wedding, and afterward had gone to his home for the wedding brunch, which turned out to be quite a social affair. Somehow in the midst of the laughter and jokes I sensed a warm rapport with this man.

Now he was trying to explain how he had gotten out to the church, hoping to pray in the chapel, and somehow had stumbled onto the telephone in the ushers' room. It had taken some tall talking to convince the cab driver he really wanted to get out to the church. After all, he had been in the bars for several days, and the cabbie was certain this was some kind of an alcoholic illusion. People want all kinds of strange things when they're full of booze. And what church would be open at that time of the night? But this friend was desperate and had heard by the grapevine that our church might be open. So out he came.

I assured him I'd dress and come down right away. But he wouldn't hear of it and insisted that if I came he would leave the church. "Do you think I'd let anyone see me in this miserable state?" was all he would say. I could only ask, "Then how in the world can I help you over the telephone?" After a long pause, there was a muffled sob. "Is there any way a fellow like me can be forgiven?" I must have come on too strong too quickly, because his response was almost bitter. "But you don't know me. I've done everything. How can I ever be forgiven?" "But do you realize how much Christ loves you? He died for you just as you are." Another pause—then, "If I could only believe that." "Ah, but you can."

Then came a hushed, choked cry, "Do you think you could pray for me?" What a moment! I fumbled for words, struggling with my own emotions, and finally uttered some kind of a cry for mercy. And then came his strained, embarrassed attempt at thanks, and a click as he hung up the phone. Then silence. There wasn't much chance for sleep after that.

This is no easy success story. The call marked only the beginning of a long, painful struggle for that man. Then one day came his yes with no strings attached, and that was when he broke into the open—a new person with all the joy and freedom only Christ can give. At first people who had known him said, as they do, "Do you think it will last?" I'm sure they said this of Zacchaeus and the woman at the well too. But Merle has gone from strength to strength as a witness in the church, a miracle of grace. The open door had not been an alcoholic illusion!

So the three-month open door experiment became the policy— a way of life for our church. That boy and that man were the first in a long and amazing procession.

There was one parenthesis in our whole experience back in 1964. We found it necessary to lock up the church for a few months at the insistence of the police, when a sick person got us into a series of bizarre incidents—a stolen microphone, gas jets turned on, a fire set, a bomb threat at Christmas time, all climaxed when our associate pastor was slugged in the dead of night. It was a strange, dark time, full of testing and fierce struggle. And our wrestling was not against "flesh and blood." After such an attack—for that's what it was—I can never again minimize the reality of Satan!

But this was Christ's church and the "powers of death shall never conquer it." [1] So the people held, stayed together, and neither suspicion nor mistrust could finally divide us. In the end we were victorious in Christ's name. What an exhausting, but amazing, exhilarating experience, preparing us, as I look back now, for greater things.

When it was all over one of our men, Don Ebert—"Ebe" as

we all called him, as refreshing a character as ever entered our doors—tossed a scrawled note into the offering plate one Sunday, "When do I get my balcony back?" For months prior to the incidents he had been using the balcony night after night as a place of meditation and prayer, struggling to hang on to his sobriety. When his note was read at their next meeting, all those faithful trustees could say was, "We'd better give it another try." Again our insurance people agreed. And again we opened the building. So the open church has really become a way of life.

And more and more it has become sacred ground after hours for all kinds of people. The carpet, especially in the chapel, has been washed with their tears—some heavy with sorrow and some light and shiny with joy. Through it all a Presence seems to brood over this place and blesses many of those who come.

Like the mortician who so recently spoke to me on our way to an interment at Hills of Rest. He leaned over and almost whispered—after all, there were casket bearers in the back seat— "Tell your people thanks for keeping the church open. I'm not one of your members, but your chapel has become a beautiful place for me. Many times I've stopped in to unwind on my way home from work, usually at two or three in the morning, and you'd be surprised who comes and goes at that hour."

But I'm not so sure I would be any more. Like coming in late one night and almost stumbling over a group of students on the floor in the chapel praising and thanking God for his goodness. I discovered this had been going on for quite some time.

Or the senior highs gathered around the communion table in the sanctuary near midnight having a great time of discussion and prayer. And this during the State A basketball tournament which always brings hundreds of teenagers to town. I had come to the church to meet Steve, who was in some trouble. Somehow he had tracked me down at a coffee party, and had called wondering if I could "meet him someplace." Yes, "the church would be a perfectly acceptable place all right." And as I walked in I thought of those words of Walt Bones, "A sanctuary . . . a safe place where anyone can come who needs help and no one can get at him," never dreaming there would be this kind of bonus—a beautiful group of worshiping teenagers.

Or the couple who came to be married. I had never met them

before, and when I asked, "Why have you come to me?" they said, "Oh, we first shared our love for each other in your chapel. We wouldn't think of being married any other place."

And over and over again people have left us a note or contacted us personally just to say thanks. So often they have come seeking for some sense of peace and forgiveness and left knowing that God is still around sharing his grace. At times it has been a bit over-whelming. Like the morning Lamont Reichelt, one of our assistant custodians at the time, came into the office all excited with a note, "Look at what I found in the chapel by the cross." It simply read, "Thanks for staying open. I came here seeking for the love of God." It was signed, "A friend."

How cautiously we had opened the door to help our own people —and ended up getting involved as we never expected. So much more than we bargained for. We had tried to say by an act, not by words, "Here we are. Available." Just that much, and people had taken us seriously. Not just the "nice" ones, but the hurting, the scared, and so often the unlovely! There was no way now we could become selective and say, "Oh no, not you. We were ex-pecting someone more respectable." But isn't that the way it is with our Lord? Whenever he sends out the invitation, the halt, the maimed, and the blind are the ones who show up. Well, the invitation has gone out and now we must live with the guests he sends us.

Like the morning the police called—it must have been a little before seven. A teenager had gotten in touch with them saying her friend was "going to First Baptist to take her life." We got to the church about the same time—the police and I and our church administrator, Steve Haas—and there were blood drippings all the way from the main sanctuary entrance into the chapel right up to the altar. There we found two razor blades. But no girl! Finally after an urgent search the police found her several blocks away crouched behind a couple of trees, trying to hide, yet desperately hoping she would be found. A bundle of misery. Her father and mother were in the midst of divorce proceedings. Her only response was, "Nobody cares what happens to me."

We could only take her to the hospital for psychiatric care as gently and mercifully as possible. No way we could turn our back on this girl without betraying our mission.

That kind of experience began to get to us. At least we were forced to ask ourselves about people. Where did they fit into the scheme of things in our ministry? Were they getting top priority? Not just the strangers, but our own—the quiet ones, the older ones, the ones who never got near the center of things but who secretly longed to be a part of it all—these too!

That didn't mean there was any great change overnight. We're much too entrenched in the old ways of organizing, meeting, and discussing for that. But at least it opened up some new possibilities. Our agenda began to get less and less manageable and comfortable. It's far easier to fix a roof or paint Fellowship Hall or rewrite the constitution than it is to deal with a sick, runaway boy or a drunken man or a desperate, broken teenager, or even with someone in our own membership who "just rubs me the wrong way."

At least Christ began to get at those precious plans of ours, making them more and more his own. This open, itinerant style began to seep into our official strategy here and there. Like the night our board of deacons took a long, hard look at the way we had been handling our "Fellowship Fund," a love offering received at every communion service. "To share a bit of hope with someone in need who might come our way," we have always said. But too much of that money was being banked, and reporting a comfortable balance at our monthly meetings didn't mean we were sharing much hope.

That night a decision was made to let loose of the money—make it available as a "cup of cold water" in Christ's name. Well, you can guess what happened. In a short time our balance dropped from about $1100 to a little over $200. But in half a dozen desperate situations a new light came in people's eyes. In one case the gas was turned on and groceries arrived in the nick of time. In another, a lift on an unbearable hospital bill was given to one of our families. And that's the way it went. We were back in business, the real business, again. "I tell you this: anything you did for one of my brothers here, however humble, you did for me." [2] No wonder there has been a hefty jump in the amount given in these communion offerings.

Here and there people began moving toward one another in trust. An open church building may not have had a lot to do with that directly. But at least it symbolized an open style. Our necks are out there and no way can we pull back without losing something very precious. Most of our people seem to be stubbornly aware of that.

That "open style" can become a part of a trustees' meeting, even when they have come together in a special meeting to deal with a vexing, snarled situation. Twelve thousand dollars was at stake, left in our custody through a court decision. There is nothing the devil enjoys more than a heated church scrap over money. No wonder these men came in all tense and anxious.

A couple of them could have really torn things up with a display of self-righteous anger, which they had a legitimate right to do. After all, why should our church pay legal fees to settle an issue which someone else had opened up? But there was more at stake than defensive feelings, and that was the unity of a Christian family.

And in some strange, beautiful way the Spirit got into that meeting. Little wonder. I discovered after the meeting that Wes Nelson, a precise, concerned businessman, had spent a sleepless night over the whole matter—much of it in prayer. That's where the battle had been won. And it was another man—the right one— Harold Wingler, who saw the larger issue and had the courage to make the right motion at the right time. Which released the money for the legal fees and made possible a couple of new ministries.

It was a liberating, healing decision. I could almost feel the powers of darkness slink out the back door. Christ had been declared Lord of some very practical matters where often we don't make room for him. That's why the meeting broke up in great joy. The way had now been opened for all kinds of creative alternatives.

This kind of victory has a way of freeing other people to become channels of communication. Like the deaconess who lingered after our first meeting this year all aglow. She simply had to report that she had "done business" with a brother deacon after a long time of misunderstanding—"ever since my son was in junior high school." A difficult, even humiliating thing to do, but forgiveness never comes at a cheap price. "Somehow" the two of them had ended up in the hall together and either she had to deal with the matter then and there or give up any attempt at being a deaconess. She was obedient. So once again new power was released among our people.

But there are other ways we have moved across the old barriers to find one another. Like our last anniversary service—a beautiful, festive time at the Lord's Table on the first Sunday of July, after a breakfast on the lawn.

Three of our people came to the Table with a fresh word for the family. First, Clint Hanson, a deacon and a clothing salesman, a member for twelve years; then Cindy Graber, a junior high who had been a Christian for one week. But it was Edna Roberts, eighty-four years of age and a member for seventy-two of those years, who gave us something very special. So alive and interested in everything going on. No one was more eager to support the newer things going on in the church. Now nervous about the microphone and her notes until she forgot and "took off," sharing some of those memories and hopes. So full of laughter and tears.

But it was her affirmation of the young that particularly got hold of us. "Most of all, I believe, I am thankful for you strong young people who have been coming into our church lately. Many of us don't always understand your language and we're confused by your noise and music. And your clothes and hair certainly seem strange at times. But I'm even getting accustomed to that. I know you love Christ, and I'm all for you!"

No wonder nine people answered the call of Christ at the close of that service. The way had been opened for that kind of response.

But how really open is the agenda, not only for the others, but for me? I kept wondering about that. Not only because of the things going on in the church, but because the men and I were having a go at the Acts of the Apostles every Friday morning at Smitty's Pancake House. I was intrigued and filled with a sense of nostalgia and longing. Wasn't this the way things were really supposed to be when the church was alive? But could we expect that today? If so, what did it mean? Not just for the others, but for me.

Or was The Acts a closed book as so many insisted? Including quite a list of respected theologians and Bible teachers. Was it just an account of God's special working back there in the Apostolic era to get that tiny Christian community launched? The world needed supernatural proofs and signs then that are unnecessary today—how many times I had heard that preached as orthodoxy all the way back to my Sunday school days.

Or was it really an "open" book—some "case studies" of what really happens whenever the Holy Spirit is given the freedom to work through ordinary people? A kind of plugging into the "Real Thing." Some instances of God's beautiful surprises whenever he is allowed to have his way. Unbreakable community among the most unlikely characters. Joy and praise that neither hostility nor prison walls could begin to stifle. Slaves and governors becoming eager witnesses that Jesus is Lord. And with a mysterious power over diseases and evil spirits through that Name. All of it like fresh wind in musty places. Had that wind really stopped blowing? I could not really bring myself to believe that. Too much of what I had seen and experienced and known recently had been a manifestation of the power of the Spirit in our time.

So I began to move through that door quietly and cautiously—testing it.

About this time a cry for help came from Merle and Sharon Johnson, a winsome, younger couple who had come into our church some months earlier. Merle had just begun a promising career as an attorney, and he and Sharon were really looking forward to the arrival of their first child. But when she arrived, unexpectedly early, there were critical breathing difficulties. It seemed the fragile little life would be choked out before she ever had a chance to get started.

It was then that their urgent call for prayer came! But prayer for what? Healing? God's will? For the mother and father if the infant should die? For what? In the midst of this wondering, an overwhelming sense of "going for broke" seemed to come over me. If the God of Acts is still alive and at work, then why not go to him expecting that he would once again breathe his life into this tiny child?

But was I trying to play hero in all this, or was this God's doing? Trembling and fearful I still held back. I knew most of the arguments for and against healing. I had read a spate of books on the subject—Emily Gardner Neale, Agnes Sanford, Bernard Martin, C. S. Lewis. I had even attended a couple of healing services conducted by Alfred Price in St. Stephen's in Philadelphia.

Yet I am also a child of a scientific age where reason has so often been the final court of appeal. A top-flight seminary course on "The Psychological Interpretation of the Gospels" had straightened me out rationally on the miracles—so I thought!

But this was no time to rehash all the arguments—only obey, as Stephen and Philip, Peter and John and the others had done. And leave it with God! So I plunged in—with sweaty hands and breath coming in short gulps, with what little faith I would allow the Lord to give me. It was a faint, struggling prayer for the little one's life. I cannot explain the mystery of God's sovereign grace. Why sometimes? And why not at other times? All I know is that the little girl lived.

Every time I see Mary Lynne around, now a lovely, maturing girl of ten, a quiet sense of joy and gratitude wells up within. The agenda is open.

It has been only in the last year that our deacons and deaconesses have affirmed the ministry of healing within our congregation—physical, emotional, and spiritual. They are willing to be involved themselves in the anointing and prayer whenever called on. These times of healing are not ostentatious "special" affairs, but a part of ongoing congregational life. Often they take place at our midweek prayer service or in a home or hospital room, as God sends people to us with needs who request this ministry. This has unfolded for us in his time without our promoting or pushing it. And we have been blessed and deepened as a people.

But even that experience with the Johnsons did not completely satisfy my hunger for God. At times it was like the ache of homesickness and at others a vague restlessness. But always a yearning, which only the intimacy of the Living God could fill and quiet. Like the haunting words of that ancient hymn,

> From the best bliss that earth imparts,
> We turn unfilled to Thee again.

But even then I moved slowly, almost gingerly. Aware of too many situations where a pastor has drunk deeply of the Spirit and then become more and more rigid about it, until he has finally begun dogmatically insisting that his own experience must be the test of everyone else's spiritual life. So people have been forced to divide up sides—"the haves and the have-nots," those who agree and those who can't—confusing and splintering the Body of Christ. Which becomes a horrible sin against the Holy Spirit. And I wanted none of that.

Yet the hunger persisted!

About this time I ended up in Brandon, Manitoba, as a speaker for a conference of the Baptists of Western Canada. I had a great deal of time alone in my motel room, which I needed, for I was doing some rather heavy reading preparing for a series of sermons on the Holy Spirit. Our people had been asking for some guidance and teaching in this whole area. In the midst of studying and seeking and praying, I was given the assurance that the Holy Spirit had filled my life. Quietly, but unmistakably! A mighty tide of joy and love flooded my life! It was as Jesus had said on the last day of the great feast. "If anyone is thirsty let him come to me; whoever believes in me, let him drink. . . . Streams of living water shall flow out from within him." [3] I could only rejoice and praise God.

And I was set free. I did not need a particular "gift" or an experience like anyone else's as a proof. The Lord was simply saying, "I have given you myself. That is the great Gift! And there is nothing more you need!" I am not arguing for a particular type of experience, only testifying that springtime came in my own life when I least expected it.

I was given new power and love, a discernment and understanding that has often amazed me. And more and more a living peace, a Shalom, has been coming into that stormy, erratic temperament of mine. The agenda is open for me—not just for the church.

Then one day we found a gift in the chapel. A cross standing on the altar, stark and alone. Terribly plain, but beautiful, made out of barbed wire and stuck in a rough hunk of wood. That said it. Marcia Julin, one of our senior highs, who had fashioned it with love and thanks, understood. People had come to this place with their prayers and their joys and their tears—even their blood —because the way was really open. The ugly wonder of Christ's death guaranteed that.

And that's what we have been trying to understand.

4.

Well,
Here
I Am

I *met Irv Harris and Bruce Larson back there in the*
early days, 1961 or so, at an unplanned, off-the-cuff luncheon in
the Princeton Club in New York City. Not the usual place for me to
eat, but I had gotten into the city for some kind of a denominational
meeting, and slipped out for a short time, hoping I could get the
lowdown on Faith at Work, which I knew about vaguely through
the little magazine. I ended up getting taken to lunch by these two
exciting fellows who were to become lifelong friends.

I couldn't have done better had I planned this meeting six months
in advance, because Irv and Bruce were at the very heart of this
new thing God had been doing in the church. And they were
eager to spill it all. Before that luncheon was over I could hear
bells ringing, and I began to catch a new vision for my whole
ministry. Something I had dimly known now began to take definite
shape.

Faith at Work, I discovered, is a fresh, living fellowship of
people eager to find God's authentic style of life for these times.
Centered in the church—not another denomination or substitute
for congregational life, as some have wrongly assumed.

This had its beginning mainly with Sam Shoemaker—one of
the gifted, creative men God gave the church in the twentieth
century. Sam had more dreams and visions in a year than most
men have in a lifetime, with an amazing capacity for seeing these

dreams through to reality. Not only did he serve two great Episcopal parishes, but he was intimately involved in the Pittsburgh Experiment,* Alcoholics Anonymous, and a half dozen other pioneering movements.

Well, Sam was strongly convinced there was a great need for ordinary people to hear about what God is doing in our time—not from the "pros," but from people like themselves. Is God really alive and at work? Or are we simply hung up on something musty and theoretical? So, typically, Sam expanded a small parish paper called *The Calvary Evangel* to tell this kind of good news in simple, unvarnished language.

He was right. His paper caught on. The whole venture mushroomed, and eventually Sam called for help. Irv Harris, his old friend at Princeton, ended up becoming the editor of this new, independent journal renamed *Faith at Work*—"the magazine of Christian experience." Eventually there were subscribers in 111 countries.

As more and more people began to read about the way Christ is at work in the lives of the Ralston Youngs and the Gert Behannas and a hundred other less known, but just as real, characters, they began to ask, "Isn't there some way we can meet one another?" So the conference life of Faith at Work was born.

These have always been semi-spontaneous gatherings with a kind of special joy all their own. All kinds of needy, hungry people have come hoping to find some kind of answer—and many have gone home by a new road. Long before the ecumenical movement had become the "in thing," these affairs were manifesting the unity of God's people in a beautiful way—Catholics and Pentecostals, Presbyterians and Episcopalians, blacks and whites, social activists and pietists, believers and doubters discovering one another in the Spirit.

As this new life kept breaking out in so many unexpected ways and places, an appeal for help went out to Bruce Larson. It was an impossible calling—to try to give some sense of direction to all this fresh, spontaneous ferment. But Bruce couldn't resist it, so he left

---

* A creative attempt to penetrate the industrial life of Pittsburgh—both management and labor—for Christ through small Bible study and prayer groups. It has become a force for renewal in that city.

the more settled life of the parish to give this new, uncharted ministry a try. And he was the right man—honestly struggling to be free himself, open to whatever God wanted, yearning for the church to find its mission again. Bruce ended up becoming the executive director of Faith at Work, but more important its visionary and catalyst.

As I sat at lunch with these two men that day, I heard about much of this for the first time and really felt at home. So it became quite natural for me to speak of my own deepest hopes and longings for the church—even my misgivings and fears. I was received like a long-lost brother, and the whole meal became a celebration. Certainly no one in the Princeton Club that day would have guessed that any kind of divine scheme was being concocted in the midst of all our hilarity.

As I heard their talk about the living thing being let loose through the witness of all kinds of scared but obedient people, I wondered out loud about the possibility of some of these people visiting Sioux Falls. Bruce's immediate response was "Why not? That is if we can get in by stagecoach!" Typical talk for Easterners! When I finally assured him we really had public transportation, even airplanes, we began seriously to make plans for a mission to Sioux Falls. Before we parted company it was agreed that Bruce would help us call together some kind of a team for a visitation to our congregation if the doors were open.

When I returned home to talk all this over with the congregation, particularly our deacons, I did not feel quite as confident as I tried to appear. The whole venture seemed far more precarious here at home than it did back in New York City. What could we possibly accomplish by importing some unknown, inexperienced lay people from all over the country for a long weekend? Could they do anything for us we couldn't do for ourselves? And why amateurs? Perhaps a thing like this would divide the church? Suppose a bunch of religious nuts showed up? And how could we possibly dig up the money to finance a team like this? This and a lot more kept nagging at me.

But in spite of these misgivings, we finally agreed to give it a try. It was quite a moment when we said, "Let's go ahead. What have we got to lose?" All part of that open agenda, now that I look back on it.

So after a volume of correspondence and a score of long-distance telephone calls—mostly with Bruce, who kept reassuring me everything would be fine—May 10 finally came. There was no way I could avoid it now. The mission was on. The team began to arrive, mostly by plane, but a few by car. To our relief they seemed quite human, not off-beat zealots or oddities at all. In spite of ourselves we began to feel more at ease.

First, there was a team meeting, a gathering of these visitors with some of our people to pull things together. We needed to get acquainted a bit, take a look at the schedule, and check our signals spiritually. And here it all came out—our fears and theirs. Which gave all of us quite a charge. They were afraid too! That was when we really became teammates. And that made it much easier to pray together—which turned out to be a living, open conversation with the Lord, who had already planned this conference, not a nervous plea for help stuck in hurriedly at the end, as is so often done at church affairs. No, as I look back on it, that time of prayer was the main part of the meeting. And it was laid out on the table—the fears, the schedule, the thanks, the whole mission. It was obvious they trusted him and expected something to happen. That was the best part of it.

Then we went to our get-acquainted supper wondering how that would come off. We knew a lot of people would be there, because our whole congregation had been invited. We would eat, and then the visiting team would introduce themselves. And that would be it. Well, it turned out to be far more than that. Not only did our friends tell about their families and their work. Each one spoke about his life in Christ in such a natural, unashamed way it almost took our breath away.

None of us will ever forget Frank Patton's telling about serving his church as a youth sponsor, a member of the choir, and even on the board of elders—"a respectable, stuffy Presbyterian," as he put it—and then making the shocking discovery that he had never met Christ. It all came out so spontaneously and humorously we didn't know whether to laugh or cry. Then through the sensitive help of a friend, Frank was introduced to Christ. It was a shattering, healing encounter that changed his life—the beginning of a whole new adventure with his family and with the men at his dairy.

Edna Roberts—
84 years of age,
and a member of First Baptist
for 72 of those years.
No one was more eager
to support the newer things
going on in the church.

Above:
The Merle Johnsons.
Every time I see Mary
Lynne, a quiet sense of
joy wells up.
The agenda is open.

Left: Janet Dewitt.
"I've tried to do it all
in my own strength.
Now I want Christ
to do it through me."

Every one of the team had some kind of a warm, real word like that to speak.

No wonder we could not help identifying with them. After all, they were like us. Frank was in the dairy business; John an attorney; Jack an English prof; Julie openly grateful to be working at being a grandmother; Bob in farm implement sales; Keith a very human pastor; Don, now with the Fellowship of Christian Athletes, had been a coach; and Bruce, our leader, was the most likeable "pro" you could imagine. And those loving, scared wives—Mellie, Louise, Marion, and Margaret—were trying to live with their husbands, help their children grow up, keep the P.T.A. going, and live with impossible schedules like everyone else. We couldn't argue with a crew like this. They were simply right for us. We even ended up with Henry Soderberg, a church worker from Sweden who happened to be in this country studying American church life, joining the team. He has never gotten over the experience.

Our visitors completely disarmed us. They made no attempt to hide their weaknesses or ignorance—or their love for Christ. There was a childlike transparency about it all. "In some unexpected, living way Christ has become the center of my life"—over and over again that was said with no apologies. Nothing sticky or false about any of it.

No one tried to cover up the difficulties of this new way. In fact, some of these friends had gotten into troubles they could have avoided had they not taken Christ seriously. "In many ways there are more problems this way because the Spirit has drawn me into the brokenness of our world. But I could never go back to the misery of my old self-centered way." That came out in differing ways.

Our strategy for those days was very simple. We tried to draw together all kinds of people in natural, informal settings where they could speak openly about things that really matter.

So some of our folks, the "entertaining kind," opened their homes and invited in members and friends and neighbors—anyone who would come. They put them at ease with some coffee and cookies, and let things flow as they would. There are some people with a gift for hospitality.

All kinds of people responded to the invitation—longtime church members as well as beginners, the ones who were seeking and those who doubted, some of the committed ones and some who had been hurt by the church, others who were curious and some who simply came along with their wives, or husbands. Great gatherings!

After folks got settled a bit, then two or three of our visiting friends would open things up. They had come to be catalysts or prompters rather than leaders. After going around the circle having people give their names and a word about family or work, they might ask each one to speak of something for which he was thankful. Or perhaps use the four "Quaker Questions" as they have been called. 1. Where did you live when you were seven years of age? 2. How did you heat your house when you were seven? 3. Who was the warmest or closest person in your life when you were seven? 4. When did God become real to you? Amazing what answering those simple questions can bring out of a group.

Usually each of our visitors would share a bit about how he had met Christ and the difference that made. Nothing preachy, just a simple word. Then they would ask for response. However they went about it, that seemed to get things moving. People seemed eager to plunge in.

The talk got really heavy at many of these affairs: "How can I know I've met God?" "Isn't prayer simply talking to yourself?" "Hasn't the church about had its day?" "Why do my wife and I find it so difficult to talk with each other, especially about God?" "Is Christ really the only way?"—and so much more! Now and then deep feelings, often pushed down for so long, would come spilling out unexpectedly, and people would confess afterwards, "I can hardly believe I said that."

Sometimes a kind of trembling silence would come over a group and folks would just sit there knowing another Presence was in the room. Quite often, hushed, honest prayer would bring things to a close.

When it was all over I was amazed to discover we had called together about forty of these small, informal groups during those days. They were of every type—men's breakfasts, women's coffees, couples' coffees, youth get-togethers—from early morning until late at night, and often two or three going on at the same time. I can assure you it takes a peculiar kind of flexibility and endurance, as well as a unique ability to consume coffee, to be a part of one of these lay missions.

No wonder the Spirit gathered up group after group and formed them into small communities of love and understanding. This was the miracle! It was like that phrase one runs into every so often in the New Testament, "Greet the congregation at their house." [1]

There were so many high moments through those days. Like the men's breakfast at the YMCA—unforgettable! After the simple, straightforward witness of three or four of our guests—and men are longing to hear that kind of talk—the room was heavy with silence. Then a chair scraped and one of our own keen men stood and after a pause, "I have something I must say." There followed a wistful expression of his own deep needs. For the fifty or sixty men present that honest cry opened the door. Man after man spoke his heart. Mistakes were confessed and the longing for new life was voiced. We left cleansed and renewed. Our men are still at it for Christ because of vows they made that day.

In my earlier correspondence with Bruce Larson, he had assured me these visiting people were coming only as catalysts for the Spirit. They would "go before the Lord" to "prepare the way," that he might bring forth what was already there. "Strange way to operate," I thought, but didn't argue the point. After all, he ought to know. My whole orientation was "I am coming to bring something to you"—inspiration, guidance, program, or whatever. "Not so," said Bruce, "let the Spirit do his work. It's his business, not your show!"

And this is the way it went. I watched in amazement while the Spirit worked his miracle through these people. He was using their weakness, not their strength. After all, these were scared, untrained lay people—and they were admitting it! And our people were soaking it up. This was their kind of language.

I wondered a great deal about their openness and response during those days. Maybe I had been robbing them of their freedom to discover their own unique ministry. For even though I spoke often of God's using human weakness—quoting Paul at this point, " 'My grace is all you need; power comes to its full strength in weakness' " [2]—when the chips were down I really wanted to live by my strength. "My plans for the church" and those "rights I have as pastor" were pretty important. Which meant I had to stay in control. So the lay people often ended up "being organized" or "manipulated" for my church program. Always in the Lord's name, of course! And that's where they were getting cheated.

This is not meant to downgrade my role as pastor. Not at all. I accept my own calling to preach and teach, to evangelize and shepherd in the name of Christ far too seriously for that. But neither is there any point in hiding my fears. I wasn't certain at all I could trust God and his people with my weaknesses and needs. Wouldn't that downgrade my "spiritual authority" and undercut my "leadership"? Could God really use my helplessness? It was so much easier to get fixed up and come with my strengths. That was my struggle. Did I dare buy in at that honest level of need and openness?

That's what I kept hearing with those lay people around. Here they were carrying on a fresh, contagious mission in our backyard. Witnesses in the apostolic tradition, getting way beyond the housekeeping chores for which we so often settle—ushering or passing out pledge cards. And I had thought they would be theologically naïve. Perhaps they didn't have the technical training, but they certainly had a trust and a spiritual wisdom which is so often lacking among us "pros." And this brought me to a decisive point in trying to understand what my own ministry was all about.

When we got to Sunday I was all set to do some kind of fresh business with God and his people—regardless of what anyone else did. There must be some way for me to begin to let loose of some of the old preacher-centered ways, stop trying to play "religious strong man," be myself, and dare believe the people would understand. Less the arranger and more the enabler—and trust that the Spirit would teach us all.

We could get into some of this right away. It would be a day-to-day style rather than a new program. Sharing life at a deep level all along the line. Taking lay people along on pastoral or evangelistic calls, even on some of those difficult trips to the state mental hospital at Yankton or those supportive appearances in the courtroom or at the Juvenile Court Center. And why not have some of the people share in some of those out-of-town speaking jaunts? And what about tying in with some of the "Peters" and "Andrews," the "Marthas" and "Marys" in the congregation who had so much to give and were wanting to be called forth and affirmed? And why not begin meeting with more small groups for study and prayer—at breakfast or lunch or whenever they were able to meet? And surely we would discover new ways to affirm and release the laity.

As we gathered for worship that Sunday, May 13, there was a spirit of holy excitement in the air. We were there to celebrate—to praise God for all he had been doing among us. You could tell it by the way people greeted one another and sang and prayed! And then Frank Patton, Mellie McKenzie, and Bruce Larson brought it all together—like bread being broken—an interpretation of all God had been saying to us during these days. The climax of it all, in Bruce's words, was the claim of Love.

At the conclusion, I could not resist speaking a word or two about what had been taking place in my own life—how this had been a time of searching and self-examination, but also of renewal and grace. A turning point in my own ministry. I wondered about the rest of our family. Did we understand what God was doing, and how would we respond?

It was a heavy moment, a time of intense wrestling, as we began to sing our last hymn, "O Love That Wilt Not Let Me Go," which had been chosen without any idea of what Bruce would say. There is only one response we can make—"I give Thee back the life I owe."

Then we came to those words, "I yield my flickering torch to Thee," and there was a shifting in one of the pews as one of our strong, gifted women moved out before the people. I do not think I will ever forget the abandon and determination of her coming. It was in her walk and her eyes. When I greeted her she could only whisper, "I've tried to do it all in my own strength. Now I want Christ to do it through me." That said it for many of us, for it is the great mystery, the central paradox, of all authentic Christian living—"the life I now live is not my life, but the life which Christ lives in me." [3] It was Janet DeWitt who had come, the one who had said in that pulpit committee meeting some years before, "We're a spiritually hungry church."

Her act of obedience encouraged others. That day a wonderful company of our people, sixty or seventy of them—deacons, trustees, church school teachers, students, seekers, and beginners—came offering their lives to God anew or for the first time. There was a deep inner response that moved all through our congregation like a wind—not confessed openly, but communicated nevertheless. What a day!

Those moments after the service were like a party. A kind of chaotic, holy affair that cannot be squeezed into words, even though we tried to understand the meaning of it all as we prayed, sang, shared, and wept together. We finally agreed to come back later in the afternoon and see if we could discover the direction we were to take.

So at 2:30 about a hundred or so people gathered in our Youth Room. I was in the unusual situation of having no agenda, with no idea where all this would end up. This had not been my way of operating. But it became the Spirit's meeting, a rich, glorious time together.

People voiced all kinds of beautiful, unexpected things. "I really came to know some beautiful people in this church I hardly knew existed before this weekend." "I just can't sit here any longer, because Christ has become real in a whole new way and I must tell you." "Believe it or not, Mary and I prayed together for the first time in fifteen years of marriage."

It was Bonnie Gerlach who really shook us up. Frank Patton had become a very special friend to her and Earl in these few days. In fact, it all meant so much to him he stayed on a couple of days longer in their home. Out of Frank's ministry Bonnie had at least begun to find a new freedom, and she wanted us to know. She had lived with all kinds of guilt feelings and hangups ever since the birth of their youngest son Greg. He had come into the world with cerebral palsy. And it was a miracle he had lived. Now Greg was a radiant, winsome guy that everyone loved (he still is—even in college), a favorite at the Crippled Children's School.

But Bonnie had been nagged and torn up by this all through the years. "What have I done wrong? Why has God punished me?" She blurted it all out that afternoon without anyone putting her down. Talk about making yourself vulnerable. And then she went on to tell us how a new freedom had begun to stir in her life. She knew now Greg was a very special gift to her and Earl.

There was one theme that kept running through all this—"Where do we go next?" "Is there some special way we can keep this spirit alive?" "Surely it's too real to die." "Can't we keep on getting together in our homes to talk and share and pray as we've done these last few days?" That's really how the small groups got underway. Not organized or promoted, but a spontaneous kind of reaching out for one another.

How could we begin to say thanks and good-bye to the amazing bunch of people God had sent our way? We tried, but there was no way. I still marvel at their spirit of abandon and generosity. When I first spoke to one of the couples about their expenses from Phoenix, their response was, "Don't be ridiculous! We should be thanking and paying you for letting us in on this." At the same time Jack stuffed a check in my pocket, and there was no way I could argue him out of it. He simply said, "There's a grace in receiving, Roger, just like there's a grace in giving." The rest of the team seemed to have caught the same kind of "crazy fever." And to think that I had worried about expenses!

Little wonder God let loose something real among us through the obedience of these people, something that continues to this day. We have been discovering ever since the cost, the excitement, and the glory of this new way.

My secretary during this time was Margy Clark. She had written the letters, kept the schedule straight, and gotten the right people to the right places most of the time—a demanding assignment! I discovered later she had written a personal summary of much that had taken place, describing her own struggle—trying so hard to force herself into this new life so she could be like the others. Frustrating business! And then several weeks later in the darkness of her bedroom she came to the end of all her effort. She could only cry out helplessly, "Well, here I am. There's nothing more I can do." It was then that a new peace moved quietly into her life. The battle had gotten her to the point where she could only utter that cry. And that was the moment of new beginning.

In some way that had taken place among many of us. We had become available. Some of us had dared say, "Well, here I am." And that is what God could begin to use.

5.

A Bunch
of
Dandelions

And years later—about thirteen—we know that visit
was no weekend jag! It was not just a spiritual high that passed
when the team packed up and took off for home. Not at all. The
power released during those days is still with us, particularly in
small group life.

We've tasted it again tonight. Ruth and I have just come home
from a really swinging time with one of those groups—at the home
of Evans and Jean Nord. We've been drenched with all kinds of
laughter and joy, and consumed buckets of coffee. How good to
welcome the Brubakers back after some months in the South. And
to be a part of some of the deep concern and prayer voiced throughout the evening. The Williams weren't there because of Jo's health,
and Lowell Hansen was back in Pierre because the State Legisla-
ture is in session.

Then we've had a real go with the rest of them at some Bible
study. 1 Corinthians 13 is where they happened to be. After reading that classic, someone blurted out, "What can anyone add to
that?" Which didn't stop one of the others from asking, "I don't see
how you can love that way. Why, I can't even handle 'love is patient.'" And Claudia put it very gently, "You can't do it yourself.
That's why it's impossible to talk about this kind of love without
Christ." From there on the talk got into family life and spiritual

gifts and how we can become more accountable to one another. Beautiful, honest stuff.

Some of the most perceptive comments came from Gale Fisher, who with his wife Claudia was with the group for the first time. At first they seemed fascinated by it all, watching and listening. Then they came plunging in.

At the end everyone stood and joined hands. And quiet, deep things were shared with one another and with the Lord. No wonder we came home with our hearts singing.

A few months earlier it looked like this group might die. But Merle and Sharon Johnson, bless them, kept hanging on and hoping for something better. Then some new people came along eager to give this kind of thing a try—Lowell and Carol Hansen, Evans and Jean Nord, Arlo and Mary Sommervold. And Earl and Bonnie Gerlach came back. That's when the group began to take off.

We had learned about this kind of life from that first Faith at Work team. Not as a technique or another program, but as one of the new things the Holy Spirit has been doing in our time. Drawing people together in small, loving, supportive communities. During their visit it seemed like every time one of our people asked, "Wouldn't it be great if this free, open style of life could continue?" one of them would answer, "It can. Like in my small group back home."

Well, that was enough. The appetite had been whetted. The curiosity and the need of some of our people moved them to give it a try. So here and there groups began to come to life. Like this one meeting at Nords. No wonder Ruth and I have come home rejoicing on other nights, strengthened and encouraged by what some other group has given us.

There was no way I could hold back on this when it got started. Only encourage it! Of course, there are risks in small group life. But then aren't there in anything worthwhile we tackle in the church? Even a service of public worship has its peculiar dangers. It can actually insulate and harden us more than save us. I think I've heard most of the misgivings about small group life. If not by pastors who wonder if they can trust the lay people, then by lay people who worry that this might rock the boat too much. "Won't these gatherings become divisive holy clubs that really tear things up?" or "What will happen to our adult Sunday school classes?" or "Isn't this another fad that will pass?" or "How can we control these groups?" I think I understand most of this. After all, I'm really an institutional church man at heart too.

But way back I had been touched too deeply by some small group experiences to let this pass without giving it a try. Particularly Alcoholics Anonymous, where I had walked into an honesty and spirit of group support that went beyond anything I had found in the church. Or the Yokefellow groups I had visited here and there, with their great sense of discipline and growth. And a couple of unforgettable stopovers at The Church of The Saviour in Washington, D.C., and a chance to join in those amazing classes in Christian living where they talked so much about "the integrity of church membership." And even our fumbling attempts to get something underway in Ottawa. And I longed for more.

I was also deeply intrigued by those references in the New Testament to groups of believers meeting in someone's home— Prisca and Aquila or Nympha or Philemon or whoever—sending greetings to other believers.[1] It must have been a wonderful network of small Christian families. This is what many of our people were longing for. So why not give it a try?

I wonder if we realize how many of our people are yearning for something real to break forth in church life. So much of the planning and committee work we carry on doesn't help much. Often it only deepens the frustration. Every once in a while someone, right in the middle of the establishment, will say ever so wistfully, "I'm so tired of all this."

Much of our worship doesn't do any better, even when we tinker with the mechanics—whether it is dialogic preaching, chancel dramas, or whatever. People still end up getting talked at while they stare at the back of someone's head. They come wanting so much and leave with so little—often untouched and even more isolated.

And how can any of those cold, thin-lipped affairs we try to pass off as church doings satisfy anyone really looking for joy and life? Not much chance to feel at home in that kind of an atmosphere. And yet Jesus kept talking about his Kingdom being like a party.

No wonder they turn to the "isms" and the sects. So many of them offer people a sense of importance and a powerful feeling of belonging. Or to the cocktail hour and the neighborhood bar where there is some kind of camaraderie and conviviality. It may take two or three drinks, but at least one can feel a part of things.

Well, the visit of these folks touched that kind of need in many of our people. This is why they responded so eagerly. And many of them eventually ended up in some kind of a group. Not only that afternoon when we asked ourselves where we were going, but in other places—unexpectedly.

Like the night Louise Lamberts spoke about her group back in Tempe, Arizona, and the love and support they were giving her. "As a matter of fact," she said, "they might be praying for me right now, because they know I'm here, and how scared I am."

Immediately the crowd meeting in that home wanted to know, "What group?" So Louise told how she and Jack had been invited to join some people who were trying to grow together shortly after they had "come alive in Christ." And what had started out as a halting, almost embarrassing, experience for this sophisticated couple—after all Jack was an English professor at Arizona State— had become a spiritual home for both of them, a place of belonging. No wonder Louise couldn't say enough about her group.

Well, you can imagine what happened. Then and there three of our couples—Len and Arlyce Perron, Gene and Evilo Loken, and Les and Cindy Hash—decided to give this kind of thing a try.

And they let us know at the church what was going on. It wasn't some secret, "Let's keep this all quiet, because 'they' might discourage us." I shall always be thankful for that. For without that kind of trust between "the office" and "the people," the pastors and the laity, we never could have survived all the group life we've been in ever since that time.

I gave them what little encouragement I could, which was mainly urging them to go ahead. No chance to program or plan this. I knew too little.

I have learned since that authentic groups are never "little churches," ends in themselves, free to go off on their own, doing whatever they please, blown about by every whim and fancy. This is always divisive and demonic, and one of the chief sins against the Holy Spirit.

No, they are a living part of the Body of Christ, responsible to it and building it up, and therefore under spiritual authority in the great biblical sense. While "lay-centered," they are open to pastoral guidance and support. So we are often called to join one of these groups for an evening to deal with a theological question or the interpretation of a biblical passage—what about the authority of the scriptures? or speaking in tongues? or the occult? or our Lord's return?

Or to help stir up once again the spiritual and psychological health of the group. People are not listening to one another as they once did. Consequently, there may have come a subtle rivalry among them and that fresh eagerness to affirm and support one another has quietly died. So there is a need to open things up again.

And sometimes we have been asked to help the group find its mission. What is Christ laying on them to do in his name?

Now this kind of pastoring can take place only in a climate of trust and acceptance. And a willingness to discern the Body of Christ. God, who is rich in mercy, has been teaching us about this over the years.

So that first group met—that first time—drank some coffee, visited a bit, and then rather shyly opened their Bibles to the Gospel of John, read a few verses and made some simple, personal comments about what they found. Then they made a struggling attempt at prayer. There were some long pauses and their hands got a bit clammy. This was all so new. Those who couldn't find any words to speak openly simply said, "Amen." At least they were with it in spirit. After everyone had taken his turn, a quiet joy filled the room. They had survived their first meeting and actually enjoyed it. As they broke up and left for home they were already making plans for the next time.

Of course, it was a cautious affair at first. They all are. Most of us have been closed up too long to "buy in" with anyone too hastily. We need time to check out the others, like they do us. And if we are pushed too much, we'll drop out. We wonder, "Will they reject me if they really get to know what I'm like?" "Will they laugh when they discover I can't even find the chapter and verse we're looking for in the Bible?" And with prayer we get even more skittish. It comes so close. "Suppose they learn I've never prayed anything but 'Now I lay me down to sleep'?" We are not about to open ourselves to anyone if we think there's the slightest chance we might be let down. I think I can understand why it was six months before Gene Loken could utter any kind of prayer openly.

But that first group kept at it and even picked up two or three other couples. And eventually things began to loosen up. They got so they could even kid one another about "that place in the Bible we're looking for" or have a good laugh when someone botched one of those unpronounceable biblical names. And a joy and a freedom began to come into their praying. More and more they began to accept one another as they were—clay feet, warts, and all!

Of course, there was pain. There always is when we get close enough to one another to become vulnerable. Like in marriage! Wayne Oates has spoken of the first year of that relationship as "the discipline of disillusionment." The awful discovery that my mate is as human as I am, and, horror of horrors, how immature we both are. That's how it is in group life. So sometimes there were tears and anger and embarrassment in that first group. Somebody was sure he was going to drop out. Only he never did. There was too much at stake. That's the story of every group that makes it!

Almost imperceptibly they began to become a family. That was the miracle—the work of the Holy Spirit. Christ became more and more the Unseen Presence—the real Host at their gatherings. In time these people discovered they were no longer a collection of individuals, but a community, a band of brothers and sisters. They had reached out to touch and accept one another and discovered they were a gift to one another in Christ. There is no need to remake one another when that happens, or to become a destructive gossip center, or a self-righteous holy club. The Spirit has taken care of that.

And so these people began to talk about "their group" just like Louise Lamberts had done. It was a kind of spontaneous overflow. Now and then someone would ask, "How do you get into one of these?" or "Maybe I ought to give something like this a try." That kind of contagious interest began to spark new groups.

So we began to noise it around, always in the last session of our membership classes and every now and then in a worship service, that we were ready to help people get started in another small group if anyone wanted to give it a try.

Whenever enough interested ones have come our way, we've

usually called them together in someone's home, often at our house. And someone like the Stapletons or the Hansens or the Brubakers —people with a gift for this kind of thing—have joined in to give a helping hand. Often this couple, these old-timers, will stay with a group, mothering it and helping it along until it's gotten launched.

These first get-togethers have usually been exciting evenings with lots of laughter and nervous anticipation. Like opening a Christmas package knowing there's something lovely inside, but not quite certain I dare cut the ribbon to tear off the paper. Who are these new, often unknown, people in this room? Can I trust them? Suppose they find out how weak and scared I am? I wonder if something beautiful and new can come out of all this? But that's all a part of opening the package.

We've kept refreshments at a minimum—a cup of coffee and a cookie—and explanation and participation at a maximum. Often we've used the four Quaker Questions. These alone will take the whole evening. Or we've spoken of one person who has influenced our lives deeply, or one exciting thing that has happened to us in the last week. And it's amazing what comes out of questions like these. A lot of laughter and often some tears!

Before it's over everyone has had a little taste of what small group life can be. After a round of prayer they're on their way home. Now it's up to them to decide whether or not they will come back the next time. Usually they do. That's when they start with some study material and begin to find their style of meeting.

It's simply amazing who's gotten into this. Some beautiful, sophisticated people like Evans and Jean Nord asking each other, when they first heard about small groups, "Shall we give it a try?" That's how they got into that "Merle Johnson group." At the very first gathering, during a time of prayer, Evans joined in, "Lord, it's been a beautiful weekend. Thanks for everything." We'll never forget it.

Or Ellen Pierce—she's beautiful too, shy and self-conscious— coming to the group for months before she ever said a word. When she did, it was like a celebration.

Or Stan Ruby, coming to us by way of The Glory House, a friendly, childlike man, now rejoicing that he was a part of a small family. And being loved without qualification by the others.

And what unbelievable combinations of people! I simply cannot explain this by the ordinary principles of group dynamics. It runs far deeper than that. It is the Holy Spirit who gathers up these odd collections of people and forms them into families of love. The lonely, the divorced, or the unmarried joining with the happily married; a worker at Morrell's with a Ph.D. faculty member; the teenager with the grandmother. Long ago I gave up trying to "organize" these groups.

Of course, we've seen some of those groups die. Whenever they have turned in on themselves, or haven't been willing to work through personality clashes, which are inevitable, or have allowed themselves to become neurotic centers of criticism, or haven't been willing to accept the disciplines of group life, or someone has dogmatically insisted on pushing a particular point of view and not been open to the teaching of the others, that group has withered away or blown up. No need to force a false success.

But we've also felt, throughout the length and breadth of the church, the quiet, deep influence of the groups that are alive.

There's been a deepened life of witness among the laity. Many of the people have been set free to share Christ spontaneously in the marketplace where he really belongs. As Merle Johnson recently put it, "The tough question for me is, 'How can I take Christ into the law office?' That's where I really have to struggle to do his will." And no preacher had better come rushing in with some glib, theoretical answer to that question. We're to be the stimulators and enablers, not the answer men. But a group of supportive, concerned lay people, struggling with the same kind of issues, can give Merle —and one another—some help. At least they will all know they're not alone out there in the heat of the battle. And that can be a real liberation.

More and more there has come a heightened sense of expectancy in our services of worship. We can all sense it—ushers, choir, pastors, and congregation. Sometimes there's a breathless hush, heavy with the promise of what God may do. People have been praying, often in their group. And now they are here, wondering, "What will he give us today?"

This kind of life has begun to seep into the formal structure of our church. The freedom and openness people have known in the intimacy of the small groups has made them dissatisfied with dreary, unimaginative board and committee meetings. So the joy of the Lord has been getting into our decision-making, the planning of our work. After all, it's the Lord's business. Why shouldn't the unexpected break forth here?

But so often it has been asked, "How long do these groups last?" Well, that first group is still alive and healthy—thirteen years later. They look forward to their get-togethers now more than ever, because in some mysterious way that "first love" remains. If you were to drop in on that group some Saturday night you would become a part of the warm, loving laughter, the unabashed talk of Christ, and the celebration of all the common little things of life.

They still kid Len unmercifully about his old baseball days and those faded newspaper clippings, and Les Hash about how lousy the city water is because he runs the city water plant, and Stape about his life as a country gentleman. And you would certainly hear about the wonder of Lenora's children, and Cindy would come right on with one of her probing, disturbing questions. That has become part of the ritual. Every group has its own. You would also catch the unmistakable sense of an Unseen Presence—for the One who has kept the group alive and growing is there!

All through these years the group has stuck to a very simple format—meeting every other Saturday night, going to one another's homes with the host and hostess leading or being in charge, with a minimum of refreshments, because overdoing the eating can kill the purpose of the group—even become a subtle contest between hostesses. And, whatever else happens, meeting for at least an hour. This frees people to leave when that's finished, although most of them stay on.

The disciplines are simple. First, Bible study. Taking a manageable chunk each time, going through one of the books, a chapter or a few verses each time, with the Gospels or the Acts high on the list. People are eager to learn, setting their own pace. (Suburbia tends to be full of biblical illiterates.) Everyone gets into the act by saying, "This is what these words mean to me," or "Here's what I think he's saying to me." There's an amazing balance or group corrective that goes on in a process like that. And there is no need to argue or push a point of view or try to convert someone else.

Then the group becomes a place of open, trusting conversation. Anyone is free to give the group whatever he wishes—his heavy doubts or sense of failure, or a great joy. Here he can unload it, knowing the others will share in it and help him carry it, and grateful that the group will receive him as he is. This becomes the healing, pastoral ministry of every group.

The group can be a place of free prayer. So many of us are used to little buttoned-down affairs with the words so carefully put together. Nice, safe, tasteless stuff with no one really expecting anything to happen. But it doesn't have to be that way. Like Mel Forseth, a heating and air-conditioning contractor, who prayed so simply in the Spirit at one of our men's noon Bible study groups just the other day. The prayer lingers with me because Mel has not always prayed this way. But this was living conversation with the Almighty. Nothing fancy, but honest, open dialogue. A phrase or a name or a longing, and much of it thanks, laid right out before God and the others! Often there is affirmation and praise which comes like music.

Increasingly we have come to see that authentic group life calls us to obedience. This has become a basic discipline. This style of life together can never become a cozy, polite exercise where people are simply taking one another's spiritual temperature! That is when stagnation and death set in, as in so much institutional church life.

No, if I know he is putting the finger on me, calling me to act, then I can grow in the adventure only if I say yes and obey. This could mean asking someone for forgiveness or taking an unwanted child into my home or confessing Christ to a neighbor or taking a stand on an issue in City Hall or becoming involved with the needs of the Indian people. That word can come to me personally and directly only if I am at a place where I can hear and obey. A group can become like holy ground before a burning bush. Then the story will become once again "the Acts of the Holy Spirit."

So we have come to see more and more clearly that mission is a part of each group's life. If the "inward journey" is authentic, it leads inevitably to the "outward journey." The disciplines of study and prayer and supportive love will move a group into the ministry of Christ.

This has led us into some suggestive, pioneering experiences recently. The teachers of younger children, some of the strong reliables in our church school, gather each Saturday morning to support one another in their calling to teach. A group of beautiful, creative workers with young people meet each Tuesday evening to pray for one another and to seek for Christ's strategy among the senior highs.

It has led to a group coming together each Sunday night to ask one another what their gifts might be. Amazing! Because all kinds of life has broken forth among the members as they have begun to discern and affirm one another's spiritual gifts which God in his grace has shared with them. And this has set many of them free. Like Margie Scott, who no longer needs to hide her longing to set poetry to music—to the glory of God. She recently blessed all of us in an evening service by doing just that.

This group, with its style of sharing, may be a clue for many others who keep wondering, "What do I have to give?" That fear or uncertainty has kept them for so long from getting into the ministry of Christ.

In that first group we have seen great power released time and again, particularly in times of crisis. Like when Lenora Bezpaletz went down into the valley with a peculiar blood disorder. It was a heavy time of darkness, a question of life and death. But her group let loose a tide of healing, sustaining, believing prayer that carried the day.

Or when Wendell and Delores Cook's twenty-two-year-old son, Allen, was killed in one of those shattering highway accidents. There was ice on the Illinois highway that morning and Allen tried to avoid an oncoming skidding car with children in it by heading for the ditch. But he couldn't avoid the truck that had also taken for the ditch to avoid that skidding car. And there Allen's life had ended. "There is no greater love than this, that a man should lay down his life for his friends." [2]

Allen had graduated from college the previous June and had married Claudia late that summer. They had had six months together.

I received the call telling me of all this between planes in Minneapolis—on my way to a ministers' conference in California. The line was heavy with the anguish of it all. When I insisted I would come home on the next plane, Wendell and Delores wouldn't hear of it. "You go on and finish out your commitment with those pastors." And there was a strange peace in their insistence—like the "Shalom" button they had found on Allen's coat after the accident.

All they would say was, "Don't worry. 'Our group' is standing by. We'll have Allen's service on Saturday when you get home." That pastors' meeting in California turned out to be the meeting of a lifetime—as though a special benediction was resting over it!

When we finally gathered for a simple family committal—before going to the church for a service of thanks for Allen's life, which turned out to be a ringing affirmation of the glory of the Resurrection, a real homegoing celebration—here stood that faithful, loving community with the Cooks, "their group." It was all there, what group life can truly become.

Well, that's the "granddaddy" of our groups, the first of about thirty now meeting. So someone could say, "Well, you can expect this sort of thing from a bunch like that. Look how long they've been at it!" But every group tastes of the same quality of life. And age or appearance hasn't got anything to do with it.

Like the "dandelions." It was Jan Pay who really got them underway. One day she came around saying, "Suppose I got some of 'my kind' of people together. Not the churchy kind, but people who have been through the mill like I have, and who know hardly anything about the Bible. And who don't want to get up-tight about how little they know. They'd be a bunch of dandelions like I am. If I got a group like that together, would you and Ruth show up to give us a little encouragement?" Well, who can turn down an invitation like that?

You have to know Jan to understand this. She is a sensitive, gifted person who came to know the power of Christ after years of fear and heartache. Grateful for every day of sobriety and peace. She kept insisting, "I'm no rose, just a dandelion. But God must love them because he lets so many of them grow and you just can't stomp them out." So dandelion it was—a suggestive, haunting kind of description.

Jan called the "dandelions" together for their first meeting in her great old brick home on Fourth Avenue. Not a typical church gathering, but all people who had gulped trouble in big doses—some alcoholic, two or three divorced, and a couple of them who had desperately tried to take their own lives. All lonely and hurting, reaching out for some kind of love and acceptance. Wondering if they could ever make heads or tails out of the *Good News for Modern Man* [3] they had been handed shortly after they arrived, but eager to learn what was in "that book." Ruth and I have seldom, if ever, walked in on as unusual and intriguing a group of people.

We opened to the Gospel of Luke. It seemed to fit with all those stories of outsiders and lost people. And the kickback was about as untheological and refreshing as I've ever heard. We had an exhilarating discussion.

Then we turned to prayer. I wondered if we ought to try it this first time, but decided to go ahead. I was certain we'd sit in an uncomfortable silence and then I'd have to bail them out with a "preacher's prayer." What terribly small faith! Because, instead out came some of the most simple, earthy prayers I have ever heard. No way I could hold back the tears, and I'm sure I heard angels singing that night.

Then Bill Alderson joined in! Talk about miracles. It was only five months since Dorothy, his wife, had been found dead on her davenport. A couple of friends who were in that circle that night had pried open the door and climbed in when there was no response for several days to numerous telephone calls or repeated beating on the door. Dorothy had been dead for a day or two, and Bill was almost gone—stretched out in a stupor. It had been booze all the way!

And after weeks in the hospital, here was Bill—not only at this meeting, but making his first attempt at prayer. "Dear Lord, I want to talk with you. I don't know if this is a prayer, but I want to talk with you. Will you give me something to do? Lord, help me to find something to do." That was when Earl Gerlach broke in, "Lord, you know I need an usher, and if Bill will do it, I'd like to have him." Then Bill turned to me—eyes wide open—and softly asked, "Am I good enough?" The answer must have come from the Spirit, "Bill, none of us is good enough to do anything. But by his grace he lets us do these things for him." There was a long, heavy pause and then, "OK, Lord, then I'll try it!" I've been in on many unusual prayer meetings, but nothing like this before.

And a week or two later here was Bill ushering at the eleven o'clock service on the south aisle in a heavy black suit—the only one he had then—on a hot Sunday in July. Nervous and ill at ease, but trying to make good on his offer to God. And as he said later, "I may have goofed up a little, but at least I never dropped the offering plate."

Well, the dandelions are still at it, three years later. Through ups and downs they have supported and helped one another—and grown in Christ's way as they have struggled to understand what Luke's Gospel is all about. Praying, laughing, and weeping together—like the other groups. That's what this kind of life is all about. People discovering that God really loves them, even though they are dandelions. And that dandelions come best in bunches.

6.

No Loitering
in the
Halls

It's not exactly the kind of sign you'd expect to find in a pastor's study. But there it is, hanging among some impressive-looking diplomas, a couple of sentimental mementos, and my ordination certificate. A saucy, neatly painted sign that reads "No Loitering in the Halls." There's even a small, blue, all-seeing eye looking out at you from the middle of the red "O." But that little sign probably says as much as anything else on that wall.

It came as a gift. A day or two after we'd gotten home from a pastors' retreat in Nebraska, here it was on my desk. There was only one person who could have possibly dreamed up anything like that, and that was Gene Christopherson. He had joined us on the retreat team almost as an afterthought.

This retreat at a campgrounds in Nebraska had been something quite special for Ruth and me. Here's where we had first met. Years before I had come to Lexington, Nebraska, to recruit students for one of our Baptist colleges. That first night in a youth camp I had been introduced to a tall, striking brunette who looked me directly in the eye, and seemed so warm and open. As far as I was concerned it was all over then. I capitulated on the spot. Although it did take a little longer to convince her—at least a few months. Ruth and I were married two years later!

So here we were, making plans to meet with those pastors after all these years, full of all kinds of beautiful memories and anticipation. Although I'm certain no one back in that camp ever suspected we would ever end up coming back to lead a pastors' retreat.

We had been asked if we might not bring some lay people along. Yes, we had said, we thought we could. So we asked around and found three other people who could come along. Harold and Lois Wingler were the first we asked. They had come alive by getting into the thick of things at the church. At first it had been some wiggly kindergarten boys and girls in the Sunday school. Quite a thing to see this strong man leading some of the little people around by the hand. Then Harold had become a deacon. And more and more we found ourselves calling on the two of them to open their home to all kinds of people—the college get-togethers or unexpected friends passing through or guests for our renewal conferences. Hospitality for them has always been a joy. Only the angels know how many have broken bread in their home.

Most recently it had been The Firehouse. We would never have gotten the coffeehouse put together in those first shaky days without Harold bringing in all those old beautiful things, a couple of wagon wheels, a wood stove, and pots and jars of all kinds, or those chairs at a special price. And both he and Lois served as host and hostess for years. They had been foolish enough to say yes.

On the side Harold auctioneers, and he and Lois run their own furniture store. So when we asked about this Nebraska thing, all Harold could say was, "I've done some foolish things, so we might as well take on these preachers."

Then Fran Stewart agreed to go along. She and her husband David were into the hairstyling business in a big way with two of David's brothers, Gordon and Roger, and their families. Fran knew all about entertaining and bridge, golf and smart clothes— but that hadn't kept her from coming to the end of all her spiritual and emotional resources. The games finally all ran out. And in a kind of broken humility she ended up coming to Christ.

It all came about so completely unexpectedly, in the kitchen of a friend, over coffee. I had shown up at this house to make a call, and here was Fran. When I entered the house she could hardly contain herself. "Imagine you showing up here. Why I've been trying for weeks to get up enough courage to call you for an appointment." I never cease to be amazed at our Lord's timetable.

There at the kitchen table she blurted out her need—a cry which our Lord never turns down. That day this lovely woman was filled with healing grace. Suddenly we knew his living Presence— and it was as if that table became an altar and the coffee the wine of the new covenant!

Fran could hardly wait for Sunday to come. She was so eager to confess Christ before the people—which she did, and David was only a step or two behind. Her baptism was a glorious affair. Now she was set free to do all kinds of new things—particularly ministering to an aged friend here and there, taking them for a snack, or a movie, or a drive. I don't know how many strung-out, needy friends, three or four unwed mothers and a couple of others coming out of institutional treatment, came to live with Fran and Dave. And this didn't cut Fran off from her country club friends—or Dave's business friends. She loved them in a new way.

She was like the Winglers. "Yes, I'm willing to give this Nebraska retreat a try—although ministers are certainly not my cup of tea."

As far as I was concerned that was our team, Ruth and I and these three. Except that on the Sunday before our leaving I ran into Gene Christopherson standing in the hall. We had seen a lot of him since he joined the family—simply hanging around whatever was going on. Before I knew what had happened that Sunday, I grabbed him by the arm and invited him to join us in the chapel for our "Nebraska briefing." And he came along, hardly knowing what was up. The next morning he was with us in the car on the way to Nebraska.

Gene had shown up at the church one Monday morning some months before, looking for a pastor, so desperately alone and nagged by so many questions. He had tuned in on one of our Sunday morning radio broadcasts. The gospel had come through and something stirred within him. So he came driving in from Baltic, a small village seventeen miles out—the target of at least a hundred Norwegian stories. He ended up spending most of a morning with Dave Mallgren, our associate. It was the beginning, and little by little this gifted, sensitive artist—for that was his work—began to move out of his cramped, hemmed-in world into the wonder of God's Kingdom. And finally one Sunday Gene came to declare openly his love for Christ.

What a day that turned out to be! As I was greeting Gene I

sensed someone else at my elbow. When I turned, here was Ruth. She had come out of the alto section of the choir to renew her pledge to Christ.

Something of all this must have been stirring in me almost sub-consciously that day when I so spontaneously invited Gene to join us. The story of who ends up getting asked and how they decide to go on one of these lay teams is full of God's surprises. This "Nebraska team" was certainly no exception to the rule.

Well, we had quite a time with those Nebraska pastors and their wives. It seemed that every time we turned around some new miracle was breaking forth. With coffee and laughter and tears lubricating about everything we did. Like Fran, who was able to move across the room in one of our sharing sessions and throw her arms around one of those pastors' wives. Such a new thing for Fran to do! This dear woman was all clutched up—"losing my son to a Catholic girl"—which to her was like the end of the world.

But Fran was able to tell her very tenderly how she, a Catholic, had married David, "a Baptist from birth." And at first there had been all kinds of reservations, "but now David's mother has become my very closest friend." "And now," Fran said, "we often close our visits together with a time of prayer. Maybe the same thing will happen to you, if you dare love your new daughter-in-law." And a beautiful peace came over this woman. That kind of thing kept happening all during that retreat.

It was in the early part of this get-together, when we were trying to get acquainted by telling a little about ourselves, that Harold Wingler pulled the show-stopper, as only he could. "You know," he said, "Gene, here, didn't have much choice about coming on this trip. He got caught loitering in the hall." When the gales of laughter finally subsided, I knew we had a phrase on our hands that was going to stick. "Loitering in the Hall." And it did. No way we could shake it. That's why Gene painted that sign and left it on my desk.

In a beautiful way that became the unofficial slogan of our lay mission teams. It represents a certain openness for us—an avail-ability that's full of holy humor, even if it doesn't make sense to anyone else. Like an "in" joke. "No Loitering in the Halls."

There would be no lay teams without that spirit of availability.

All those fearful, shook-up people who have wanted to back out at the last minute, but have somehow managed to see it through. Who have come home jumping up and down with excitement, bursting to tell anyone who will listen about what has happened. The biggest surprise is usually, "Imagine, the Lord used even me!" There have been all those priceless times when a carload of slightly delirious people have pulled up at our house—usually late Sunday night or in the wee hours of Monday morning—banging on the door, wanting to dance and sing because they have seen Christ at work, especially in their own lives. I wouldn't have missed that for anything!

It all started so simply. Not in a committee or a planning session, but with an invitation, and a hunch I couldn't shake. But most of all it was the obedience of four lay people. I had been asked to lead one of those post-Easter preaching missions in Topeka, Kansas. Most ministers have tried that at least once. But this time an interesting possibility kept running through my mind. "If that Faith at Work bunch could come and share with us, why can't some of our lay people join me on this mission?" So I tested the idea on Jim McCrossen, the eager, young pastor of that church. He was game. As he wrote, "After all, we don't have anything to lose."

So I went down on Sunday, "the star" of the mission. After all, my name was on all the posters. And "the helpers" joined me on Wednesday. Only by Saturday all that had changed. I have always felt a special sense of kinship with those four people, really pioneers who dared take that first chance. Len Perron, a hardware salesman and a deacon, an intense, dedicated Christian, eager to be Christ's man. We had been through some great times calling together. His wife Arlyce, an open, loving person who had really thrown her all into our Sunday school program.

And Al Piorier, an industrial implement dealer. He and I and a couple of other fellows had gone up to hear Billy Graham preach in the Minnesota State Fairgrounds some years before. In the hushed darkness of our dormitory room later that night Al had spoken shyly, almost like a little boy, about his commitment to Christ.

Some weeks before we left for Topeka, I had heard Lenora Bezpaletz, a homemaker and a registered nurse, share beautifully with a group of senior highs how Christ is really alive and can be a part of all life—particularly nursing. Well, these are the four who went.

They came on scared, but real. Nothing canned or professional about what they said or did in the coffees, evening sessions, breakfasts, group meetings, or visiting with folks one by one. And the people responded to them just like we had responded to the Faith at Work team a year or so before. Our "team meetings" were mainly times of trying to figure out what to do next—and trying to hold one another up. I don't know when I've heard as much fervent prayer—beautiful times of really laying hold on God's power.

There was the evening when Arlyce was to share a word. Standing on the platform during the song service she was almost gray with apprehension, and finally leaned over and whispered, "I don't know if I can make this. Maybe you ought to skip me?" All I could do was try to give her some kind of word of encouragement. "Well, hang on and try, and if you simply can't we'll let it go." And pray!

A moment or two later the pastor asked the congregation to sing "Christ the Lord Is Risen Today." It was really "out of season," because Easter had passed. But it hadn't! As we started to sing Arlyce was released. I could almost feel her burden lift physically. Once again she whispered, only this time it was, "Everything is

Hospitality
for Harold
and Lois
Wingler
has always
been a joy.

Gene Christopherson
got caught
standing in the
hall and went
with us to the
Nebraska pastors'
retreat.

It's an
unfinished
story, as
people keep
getting tapped
in the halls
to go out
and share
their faith.

fine!" And it was! Her witness came through clear and fresh, and people were deeply touched.

And that's the way it went. The Spirit took the fearful, weak—but obedient—offering of each of those people and used it powerfully. That's the whole story of our lay witness teams.

By Saturday I knew I should really turn things over to them and start for home. If I stayed around now I would simply get in the way. No need for me to put the finishing touch on things or to assume they couldn't make it without me.

When I suggested this in a team meeting there were some mild protests. But deep down I knew they were willing to tackle it. So they took charge of the Saturday night groups and handled the sermon time on Sunday morning. And it turned out to be a beautiful climax. All kinds of people confessed openly a new eagerness to get with it for Christ. Our four came home like the seventy Jesus sent out—full of joy! Ruth and I will never forget the way those four came crashing into our house late Sunday night. They had to tell someone how they had seen God at work.

I was thankful for the chance to drive home alone. With all this excitement churning in me I needed time to think, to sort out what was really going on. We had really stumbled into something big. I had watched four of our ordinary, "straight" people get turned on to become unashamed, spontaneous spokesmen for Jesus! Not because they were particularly talented or had been given special training, and not without a lot of nervous fear. But because they had dared obey. And that's what God had used!

They had gotten out on a limb far enough so they simply couldn't make it without some "Real Help"—and the Holy Spirit had empowered them to be his witnesses. That's the story of Pentecost and the Acts that follow!

But then, I kept wondering, why couldn't we let more of this happen? We could, but then I would have to stop protecting our lay people, letting them settle for nice, safe chores. I was back on that again. I would have to help get them into the big thing on the agenda. Which was sharing the Good News. Becoming witnesses. And that was the crucial, burning mandate of Christ.

By the time I got to Sioux Falls I knew that if any more opportunities like Topeka came along we would grab them with both hands. And that's exactly what happened. Good news has a way of getting around. Len Perron told a hardware dealer in Dell Rapids about what he had seen God do in Topeka. It wasn't long before this man's pastor called. He had heard about the Topeka lay team experience. Was there any chance we could send a team to this church? Well, we could certainly try. And so a team went up to this town nineteen miles away with Len Perron as "team captain." There was already a bit of lingo emerging.

It was a different kind of experience. When these folks discovered there weren't any small group meetings arranged for Saturday afternoon they asked about calling on some of the shut-ins. Nothing rigid or locked in about what they had come to do. They were eager to encourage the church any way they could.

But a quiet miracle was let loose in this reserved, Scandinavian community. In the morning service Charles Stapleton asked if he might not speak a word. He ended up confessing Christ openly for the first time. He had joined the church eight years earlier to please his wife and "to be a good example to his children."

But then "Stape" had lost his ten-year-old son, Robbie. It was congenital heart failure. He was riding his bicycle one Saturday evening and simply crashed to the ground. That was it. Even mouth-to-mouth resuscitation didn't help. And up until then Stape had felt he could manage almost anything. But not this! So there came an awful night of helpless despair.

But finally one day on his rural mail route he stopped the car and offered up that painful prayer of surrender. "OK, God, you can have him. If peace can come by believing like they've told me, then here I am." Peace did come. And Dell Rapids was the first place Stape had to confess it.

Well, that humble statement opened the flood gates. The host pastor, Herman Van Arsdale, then stood up and shared his needs— his sense of failure and his longing to know God intimately and his desire to be a better pastor. And others followed. It was a healing, cleansing climax.

No wonder "Van" called me that night so excited I could hardly understand what he was saying. Later he wrote, "I am truly at a loss for words to describe my feelings and the feelings of my people about the marvelous working of God in our midst during the few days your people came to share with us. We have seen anew the truth of the Scripture, 'Not by might, nor by power, but by my Spirit, says the Lord.' [1] The glory of it for us is that this has happened right here in our church in Dell Rapids." Nineteen miles away.

Next it was Akron, Ohio—about nine hundred miles. Merle Brubaker traveled all that way with "his" three women—his wife Evelyn, Bonnie Gerlach, and Gladys Gardner—hardly knowing what they were up to at all. But they were the only ones we could get to go all that way. And once again beautiful things happened. A pastor was encouraged and the people in that church began to see new possibilities. And these four are still laughing about how they ran out of gas on the Ohio Turnpike.

Just a few days ago a letter came from a layman in that Ohio church. In part it reads, "Greetings. . . . I am writing to tell you about an event our church will celebrate at a dinner banquet on January 11, 1974. The reason for the celebration is that it was ten years ago, on September 4, 1963, that a team of laymen from your church came to be with us as a 'Faith at Work' team. During the five days they were here they witnessed their faith and introduced us to the importance of fellowship sharing groups. From that beginning we have many groups that meet in homes and at church during the week. At present we still have five active groups that meet. . . . Through that visit many of us have grown closer together as Christians and have deepened our knowledge of the scripture."

And that after ten years, from the rubber capital of the world! Well, back to the beginning.

After Topeka and Dell Rapids and Akron we were off and running. It was almost uncanny how the invitations started coming in from places like Wellington, Kansas; Rapid City, South Dakota; and Lansing, Michigan. We even had one brave team that got to Scandinavia with Stape as the captain. But that's a book in itself. At first we discussed very carefully whether or not we could handle three or four assignments like this a year—or possibly five. But as greater freedom has come we've dared tackle ten or twelve missions a year, and last year it was sixteen. It hardly seems possible that 362 of our people have been involved in 137 of these missions in twelve years, all the way from Vancouver, Canada, to Mansfield, Ohio. And we have never sent out a promotional folder—only a mimeographed interpretation with some simple guidelines for those who have contacted us wanting information.

As we have gone along, a simple, flexible strategy for all this has emerged. We quickly came to understand that these missions must be the burden and joy of all our people, not just of the pastor and a few handpicked leaders. Then all we'd end up with would be some "professional lay people" going out telling the same hackneyed story. And eventually that would mean stagnation and death.

No, what we needed was the strategy of that early church in Antioch. Barnabas and Saul had gone out because of the Spirit's thrust, and that was the business of the whole congregation. It was an act of obedience. "While they were keeping a fast and offering worship to the Lord, the Holy Spirit said, 'Set Barnabas and Saul apart for me, to do the work to which I have called them.' Then, after further fasting and prayer, they laid their hands on them and let them go." [2]

So we set these missions at the center of the deacons' business. Here is where the request for a team is first heard, discussed and usually accepted—prayerfully and gratefully. That acceptance depends upon the urgency and honesty of the request. Does the asking church understand that we can only come in weakness and simplicity just as we are, and not as experts to solve their problems; or that this is not another program to add to the calendar?

It is quite a thing to hear a request considered at one of our meetings and then have it affirmed, usually unanimously with a spirit of expectation.

Then a Lay Witness Committee—which is really a task force—picks up the details. First is finding a team captain for this particular mission. That's crucial, because the captain must be a sensitive, open kind of person who understands how and why we are going and is eager to give it a try. Then helping that person find teammates—a couple or two, an older person perhaps living alone, a high school or college student. A whole book could be written full of surprises and cliff-hangers—and fervent prayer—about how people have "decided to go."

Like Mrs. Floy Van Ausdall, a *grande dame* in the classic tradition, who had surprised and delighted us all by deciding to go to Monmouth, Illinois. She was eager for the experience. But late the night before the team was to leave she accidentally discovered that she had been a day off in her calculations. It was Thursday morning at five they were to leave instead of Friday. A person half her age would have dropped out at that point. But not Mrs. Van! She simply hurried home, got her things together, was ready to leave by five a day earlier, and had the time of her life.

Or Glenn Muetzel, a hog buyer at Morrell's, who couldn't bring himself to say "yes" to a mission to Mansfield, Ohio. "After all," he kept telling himself, "the boss won't let me off." But there was an inner pressure he couldn't shake. So he finally put it to the boss in such a weak, fearful way that it's amazing he even listened. "They've got this crazy thing going at our church—laymen going off to tell other lay people about their faith—and they want me to go along. But I'm sure this is not the time for me to be gone for a couple of days." But even that much in the stockyards meant taking a stand. And to Glenn's utter amazement the boss gave him two days off. No excuse now.

When he returned, all choked up with the excitement of the weekend, his fellow workers were eager to get the full scoop during the Monday morning coffee break.

And as his story came spilling out, all of a sudden Glenn became aware how intently the men were listening. Then he realized, as he told us later, that a witness was being made, and, wonder of wonders, he was the one who was the spokesman. He knew, then, that God had more of his men at Morrell's than he had ever realized.

Well, this book could be full of stories like that!

But there are other details. What kind of a schedule will that host church work out? Is there a spirit of imagination and expectancy in their planning? What about the Friday night get-acquainted supper? So often the members of a congregation scarcely know one another beyond the casual weather-talk level. And much of this in smaller churches where the pastor so often says, "Oh, the people here really know one another." But they don't!

And what kind of a men's breakfast will we have Saturday morning? And the small group coffees throughout the day—will they be the usual cozy, church get-togethers with the same old reliables? Or will they be exciting gatherings with some seekers on hand where new things can break forth? And will the host pastor "let go" of the Sunday morning worship so these untrained visitors can speak out of their hearts? Most of the time the pastor and the church are open to this kind of thing or they wouldn't have contacted us in the first place.

Then we have to find out if our expenses will be cared for. And will the hospitality for our people be cared for in some imaginative way? Often the miracle of a weekend has broken forth after hours when our people have gone to their assigned homes for the night.

The team briefing before our people take off is something special. Everyone is a bit nervous and excited. "What will it be like?" "Why did I ever say yes to this?" "I have nothing to say." But eager too! Of course, we go over the details of the mission as best we can. But more important, this is a time of affirmation, of "buying in," so that a group of people becomes a team. Often we lay our hands on these witnesses as we give them and the whole weekend to God. And more and more our whole congregation has become a part of every team going out.

So they go and they come. And our memories and files bulge more and more with all kinds of beautiful happenings—as well as a painful failure here and there. We have had more than our fair share of laughter. Like Lamont Reichelt going to Lansing, Michigan. A retired farmer and a man of very few words, Lamont had surprised us all by his sudden decision to be baptized, and that in his late sixties.

He had agreed to go to Lansing if he didn't have to say a word. "Let the Missus take care of that." But in spite of himself Lamont got into the swing of it and ended up taking part in the morning service. He stood there gripping the pulpit with both hands and finally the words came, "If there's a door up here I'm going to get out." But he didn't—and when the friendly laughter died down, the people wept with him as he told of Christ's presence in his life.

Only Bob Olson and Merle Johnson on the same team could end up sending us telegrams on their way home from Kansas City. First one came from Auburn, Nebraska, sent at 6:58 P.M. on December 8. "Mission was big hit. Traded cars for tent and truck. Going on road. The Team." Then a second one came from Sioux City, ninety miles away, sent at 10:17 P.M. the same day. "Opened tonight in Sioux City. Tremendous collection. Purchased calliope. The Team." Needless to say we've framed these and put them among our collection of special trophies.

But most of all we have been stretched and renewed as these teammates have come home with new fire and joy in their lives. This has been far more than an emotional jag which has drained off after a few weeks. Many of these people have brought new lift into our boards and committees, or our worship and teaching, or out into special places of need and service in the community. I am certain we would never have tackled the budgets of the last two years with their hefty "faith gaps" had it not been for the people on the budget committee who had come to a new understanding about faith on one of these missions. And so often these have been the quiet, strong, faithful ones—not the ones with the dramatic Damascus road experiences.

Like Oliver Clark and Mildred Scott—an Andrew and Martha in our church—always there whenever needed. In some wonderfully unexplained way they ended up on the same team bound for Menlo, a very small Iowa community where there are a couple of rural Methodist churches. Oliver had been a deacon, had served on the church council and half a dozen committees. He had always done whatever the church asked him to do. It was his duty. Likewise Mildred. She had done most everything in the Women's Mission Society and had worked in the church kitchen since the year one. Somehow these two had gotten caught "loitering in the hall" and felt they had no legitimate excuse. So they could only say yes even though this was a strange new thing.

But something happened to these two in Menlo—unexpected and beautiful—a new tenderness and openness came to them. Grace rather than law. Without knowing any of this I called on Oliver to say a few words in the Sunday evening service. No chance for any briefing because he and Alvina had come in after the service started. Well, he came quietly to the front, stood there for a moment—and then blurted it out. "I can't quite tell you what has happened. All I know is that after belonging to this church for thirty-seven years I've discovered God loves me." There was another long pause as tears came trickling down his face. And that was it! He simply walked back to his seat. But Oliver has never been the same. And he speaks of Menlo as the place of his new birth. Imagine that, after all those years!

It was the same way with Mildred. We all noted a new eagerness and love in her, a greater willingness to accept people as they are with their clay feet and shortcomings. And then her chance came in a Sunday morning service years after Menlo. She stood there that day with a voice choked with emotion, clinging to the pulpit, and told us how she had been in the church all her life, as had her folks, and she had done all the things you were supposed to do. But now there was a new power and joy in her life and she was eager to do her Lord's bidding. It was a whole new way of life. And this had its beginning at Menlo. What a moment!

Well, it's an unfinished story. As people keep getting tapped in the halls and say yes, new chapters are written with no ending in sight. Now other churches have joined us, and they are sharing their life with others.

7.

It Just
Doesn't
Make Sense

But why go to Akron or Dell Rapids if we really hadn't gotten it all done at home? There were throngs of young people all around us, most of them, as far as we knew, untouched by any church. They came from places like Parker or Beresford hoping to get into something in the "big city"—one of the two colleges or nurses' training or one of the two hairstyling schools or the business college. And lots of them to find jobs. No wonder KELO radio reported, on the basis of a marketing survey, that the average age of our community was 24.5 years.

Many of these young people were on the move, restless and wondering, trying to find their place. You could meet all kinds of them any night at Pappy's or the South Gate Tap or Charley's or at one of the other watering holes on South Minnesota. Convinced for the most part that the church was in no way a part of their world.

So here it was. A great, untouched opportunity right under our noses. What could we do about it, if anything? Discuss it and make another try at beefing up the old, stereotyped churchy approach? Or was there something bigger on God's agenda? How could we drive a stake right in the middle of all this—not on the edge of it—and claim it for Christ? Was there some real, living way we could make ourselves available to this crowd? That's what we decided to do. In February of 1967 we launched a whole new ministry. That's when we opened The Firehouse.

Once again it really crept up on us. No one expected anything to happen that soon. After all, we had been talking about "our great opportunity among the young people" for so long, certain it would take "quite a while" to get anything underway.

But then one cold December day we came on a sign—"For Sale or Lease. Call 336-2570, Tom Costello, Jr."—stuck in the snow at 22nd and Minnesota, one of the busiest corners in Sioux Falls. It was outside the most intriguing building you can imagine—an evacuated fire station, brick, Spanish colonial, with a great plate glass window on the front. I have no idea how long the sign had been standing there, but that day all the bells started ringing. It was almost as if the Lord were saying, "Here is the place, all waiting and ready."

I could hardly wait to get downtown the next day to check this all out. Rich Gorsuch, an artist and an ad man—and a beautiful new friend in Christ—came along. He had a feel for these kinds of things. Although I'm not certain he understood my eager babbling too well. Then we stopped to take a look, pressing our faces against that dirty plate glass window like a couple of kids at a candy counter.

Well, it wasn't what we saw so much as what we felt it could become. Glowing lamps on brightly decorated tables with waiters and waitresses eagerly hurrying around with coffee. And the place full of people and laughter and music. It was all like a party. I'm certain Rich understood this.

There was no way we could leave without giving some kind of thanks to God. Rich was so new at this Christian thing that I'm sure he must have wondered, but he never let on. So there in the snow we praised God for what he was going to do in this evacuated building.

The more we learned, the more it seemed this place was ready and waiting for some new mission. The city had sold the fire station when the fire department had moved out to two new locations. Three aggressive businessmen had picked it up as a sideline and turned it into a Suzuki City, confident the motorbike business would be a surefire moneymaker. So for a couple of years the place had been full of grease and smoke and the roar of motors. Then there had been a sharp division of opinion among the three, even some ugly feelings, and finally a split. So they were trying to get out.

That's when we came along. Naïve Christians taking on what apparently had been a failure. Another case of lambs among wolves. The terms were stiff—a year's lease at $450 a month, unless we bought it. And we were in no shape to do that!

Over coffee, while all this was being discussed, something very beautiful was taking place. For the man giving us the advice was watching and listening ever so carefully, and suddenly he blurted out, "Rich, I feel there is something different about you. You don't seem to be the same old cocky so-and-so I used to do business with." Rich could only reply, "Well, maybe so, because something pretty important has happened to me, and that's really begun to shake things up. But I didn't know it showed that much." When the other man asked, "What's that?" there was a pause. And then, "Well, I haven't really talked much about it. But I met Christ, and if there's a difference, he's doing it." The first man could only say, "You know, Rich, there is a difference, and I think it's great." Then there was a glad joining of hands. Another one of God's surprises!

The next day Bob Veninga, our gifted youth pastor at the time, and I decided to call a meeting to check this all out. It was one of those ad hoc, spontaneous affairs, quickly called because there were deadlines, and we had to get the feel of the people who would really give it to us straight. Two things I remember about that meeting—it was fourteen degrees below zero, and eleven brave souls showed up. We had tried to pick out a cross section of dreamers and realists, and they came. There wasn't too much to get enthused about in that dirty, cold, dreary place. Those motorbikes had certainly left their mark. I remember wondering, "Why in the world did we call this meeting?"

Well, as we stood in a circle and shivered, Bob and I tried to lay out our dream as quickly as possible. Here were all these young people moving around our end of town with no place to light except in those night spots. And they weren't about to touch a church with a ten-foot pole. We at least ought to offer them an alternative.

Well, why couldn't we surprise them? Outflank them? Dress up this beautiful old building and make it into a coffeehouse. Turn it into a party place in the name of Christ. What would happen

The Firehouse—
a place of warmth and
love for all kinds of
people.

One cold December day we came on a "For Sale" sign outside an evacuated fire station, brick, Spanish colonial. Rich Gorsuch and I stopped to take a look, pressing our faces against the plate glass window like a couple of kids at a candy counter . . . visualizing what we felt it could become.

if some real, unafraid people were on hand night after night simply to welcome anyone who came and serve them coffee? Couldn't this become a "Firehouse"—that's the name we threw out, and it stuck —full of the warmth and light of the Holy Spirit?

Well, the excitement picked up a bit then. And as these dear friends—what else can I call them?—began to move around to look things over, they even voiced a dream or two of their own. "Here is where we could have the kitchen," or "We could have a lot of beautiful art up here in this 'upper room' "—and that name stuck too—or "With the right kind of decorating we could really give this place a fire station effect." And right in the middle of all this one of the most practical men of the lot—Ray Swift, a contractor— spoke up. "I believe a fellow could run a pipe in here for a sink." You have to know Ray to understand what that really meant. Somehow I believe we knew then it was going to take off and go.

Then another great fellow, a very unsentimental cattle buyer, Del Greenlee, let his feelings out. "This really doesn't make a lot of sense, but then nothing much else we do around the church does either. So maybe we ought to give it a try." Beautiful, prophetic words. By that time, even though we were almost frozen, we agreed to meet again, closed with prayer, and went home to think it over.

The next time was in a much warmer place, the parlor of the church, with some very important new recruits. After some heavy discussion we agreed to push ahead and give The Firehouse a try. That was after Harold Wingler told about a very special deal on some chairs. "Seventy good, hard oak ones at $4.10 apiece if we take them now." It was Del Greenlee who then said, "We'll take them." When someone more cautious tried to slow things down, "But we haven't even got any money in the bank," Del's answer was very direct—"I say let's take them." That ended the matter and saved us from all kinds of headaches. And that is one of the reasons Del ended up as our first board chairman.

We agreed to "travel light." There was no other way. Which meant that all our arrangements were made so tentatively that we could get out at the end of three months—if we weren't making it— with a maximum investment of $1500. Even Mr. Costello got in on the act a bit by giving us a special lease option at $350 a month for those first crucial ninety days. Each of us who was willing became liable for his fair share of that $1500. That's when we found out who was really "buying in." Too bad the church isn't willing to take more chances like that.

Before that meeting ended every one of us had gotten on a task force. That's the only way we were going to get it done. Cleaning and decorating—that was a big one. Handling the lease and financial matters, moving a couple of walls, getting the sink and refrigerator and stove installed and the plumbing and furnace in working order, building tables and finding some really distinctive coffee mugs. That's only part of the list—quite an assignment with opening less than two months away.

Oh yes, we had coffee at that first meeting—a very special brew that Maureen Knight had prepared. It was agreed, then and there, that she would have to dig up some esoteric, way-out recipes and try them out on the rest of us at later meetings. Which she did, and ever since she's taken a lot of razzing about all those special coffees—especially what came to be known as the "Firehouse Frankenstein." But we never had to call a doctor!

Then the miracle began to unfold. All those people carrying in that old beautiful stuff to give the place atmosphere—a couple of old wagon wheels to be finished and hung as light fixtures. It was one of our blind friends, Sue Harrison, who paid for the lovely lights on those wagon wheels out of her meager income. A lovely, black wood stove; a quaint, old-fashioned cash register; a great heavy bar for coffee serving; all kinds of pots and jars for those shelves in the front window; even an old wooden bathtub for the men's room downstairs. Finally there was a great silver bell on a stand which had that real fire engine sound! Gloria Evans and her friends had a knack for digging up all that kind of stuff and getting it hauled in.

The lights burned into the wee hours night after night as the heavy cleaning and carpentry and painting went on. All kinds of eager, inexperienced people—many of them college students—got into that. But it was Don and Peggy Basham who put it all together. They were a gift to the whole venture—a marvelous team. None of us will ever know how they managed to give away all that time, day after day, and still hold their family together and get their regular work done.

They had come from Virginia, and their soft Southern talk really stood out in our Scandinavian country. Don was the head engineer at the V.A. Hospital—a great bear of a man, tender and tough, with all the know-how we needed. And Peggy was really his partner.

Maureen kept brewing her coffees, three or four kinds, working out a menu and finding "coffee makers" who would serve on the crew. Then she managed to uncover some of the loveliest cups and saucers that beautifully fit the whole scheme. And she got hold of some gay, flowery oil cloth table cloths with lovely red lamps for every table. That warm glow was starting to come.

We never seemed to run out of surprises. One of those Suzuki businessmen had growled at us that he didn't want to be any part of a "missionary project" when we were dickering with him about lease arrangements. But he ended up giving us a great stereo sound set.

Then Ray Swift brought in his gift, a beautiful hand-carved panel for the front door—a dove and a flame and the word "Firehouse." The work of his own hands. That seemed to say it all. And all this in less than two months!

The recruiting and training of waiters and waitresses was another story. Amazing! All kinds of people showed up eager to give it a try—young and old, rich and poor, everything from Catholics to Congregationalists. And, of course, lots of our own. They were as nervous and excited and ignorant as Bob Veninga and I—and we were supposed to be the experts. These training sessions were mainly trial-and-error affairs—full of laughter and good-natured banter. We shared the dreams, tried to agree on some techniques for serving coffee without spilling it, talked about keeping our money affairs straight, and tried to put people at ease about mingling freely with those who might come our way. And spent considerable time on what the "inner journey" could mean each night. This was to be a half-hour of "centering down," a spiritual preparation for the "outer journey." We worked at all this together.

But the deeper issue was whether everyone knew why we were going into business. Would this end up being simply another coffee drinking place, nice and interesting, but really a competitor with the commercial restaurants for the coffee trade? Or something more?

So we had to ask how we could help let The Firehouse be a place of meeting, where open, trusting relations might be kindled.

Where we could hear and understand and affirm one another and all those who would come our way. Where we could all be ourselves, ask our questions, speak our doubts or failures without being put down. And be willing at the end to do business with Jesus—knowing that he is always there to heal and forgive and make new—the fulfillment of all our seeking and greater than all our needs.

This meant if we worked we were committed. Every time we opened the door we would be on display. No way we could avoid it. Not in an officious, programmed way, we hoped. But in a quiet, tender way. By the way we greeted those who came, and the way we handed out the menus or brought in the coffee and the pastries, or visited with those who wanted to talk. In all this each of us would be saying either, "I am with you in the marketplace, available and open, your friend," or "I'm afraid of you and the less time I have to spend with you the better. So let me hurry and serve you and get back to my own safe group at the corner table."

We couldn't pull off this kind of ministry with resolutions or guidelines or rules. Not a chance. That wouldn't get us through the first week. No, here we were dealing with something far deeper. We were asking ourselves about commitment and surrender and life in the Spirit, which is ambiguous but very real. And always a gift, an act of grace, received only by the humble and childlike. That meant there was no way we could avoid doing business with Christ, because he is the great issue! And without him there would be no Firehouse.

Well, how could we let all this happen without getting pushy and manipulative, driving people away with the hard sell, or on the other hand backing off from the real issues and watering everything down so that it all becomes mushy and nothing happens? We've struggled with that issue ever since we opened. And we've failed both ways at differing times.

After all our talking and planning and praying, we finally divided up into crews, or teams as we now call them, ten to twelve people for each night, named our hosts and hostesses, and braced ourselves to open the doors. Oh yes, we did call everyone together the night before so that we could all greet one another at one time—a great, beautiful bunch of people—drink some of our own coffee, and just celebrate! None of us will ever forget the quiet words of hope that

Gloria Evans and Del Greenlee spoke, nor the litany of dedication:
"How wondrously God has led us to this place which we now call
'The Firehouse.' The very possibility of the structure, the fire
engines that once were housed here, even the failures of other
businesses, all seem to have been a kind of strange preparation
for this to become a Coffee House of love and grace. So this is to
be a place of fire where the warm glow of light and warmth will
be known," we read together. And then again, "There must come
to all of us a new depth of love, honesty, and concern not only for
ourselves and one another but for all those whom God may bring
our way—the seeking, the angry, the doubter, the indifferent, the
curious—as well as the Christian friend. So we long for this to be
a place of love."

Then came our first night—February 15. We were like excited
children on the eve of Christmas, wondering, would anyone come?
And would we know what to do if someone did come? Then we
entered into our first inner journey—a kind of nervous, but real,
time of sharing our hopes and fears. We were just finishing our first
round of prayer when there was a loud knock on that beautiful
front door! So we hurriedly finished before those first customers
would have a chance to leave, unlocked the door, rang that silver
fire bell, and cried out, "The Firehouse is now open"—which was
to be part of our ritual each night.

We need not have worried about those first customers leaving.
They were a foretaste of all who were to come. They've been
knocking ever since—approximately twenty thousand a year now
for almost eight years with no sign of let-up. Almost unbelievable!

That first night was a celebration, an affirmation, a beautiful
acceptance of what we had set out to do. With all kinds of "oh's"
and "ah's" about everything—the paintings, the coffee mugs, the
cash register, the purple color scheme of the women's toilet, the
menus, the wooden bathtub in the men's room downstairs, and
most of all the spirit and style of the place. It was all great—
almost too good to be true!

That's the way it went. Word got around. Plus the fact that we
passed out fifteen thousand invitation cards in all kinds of unlikely
places—at the motels and the bars, at the country clubs and the
colleges and those other training schools. We wanted to get outside
the churchy ghetto. So more and more people began to show up to

look things over—after a play or a concert, students after games or parties, and some even after church affairs—enough sinners among the churchy to keep it all healthy and well balanced, we felt.

Some nights there were great, rousing sing-alongs. Lynne Larson at the piano or Joel Engelland with his banjo could always pack them in. And we discovered all kinds of beautiful singing groups—from the University and South Dakota State as well as from town. Wally James, a professional guitar player, "gave" us Sunday nights for months. And Rae Engles made her comeback, or debut, whatever you want to call it, after a long siege of mental illness, singing stuff like "Soon It's Gonna Rain" and "Just in Time." An almost unreal hush came over the crowd that night. People seemed to sense that something very special was going on.

Gloria Evans changed the art every two or three months, and every once in a while somebody unexpected showed up asking if they could read some original poetry. Mary Husby helped us a lot with that. We always left that up to the host and hostess. And occasionally someone showed up to lead in a discussion—Larry Baulch, the author of *Return to the World*,[1] or the candidates for mayor of our city.

The pastries kept coming in from all kinds of people under the encouragement of Olive Cressey first and then Catherine Wartenhorst. Donated! Catherine's husband George became our unofficial handyman, keeping the chairs and a lot of other things in repair.

Wes Nelson and then Arnold Petersen served as our faithful treasurers, trying to give our ragged finances some semblance of order. At best a challenging undertaking.

So you could drop by any night and get the feel of the thing we had talked about at the start—meeting and openness and acceptance. It was all there! Those crews were something. Grandmothers like Mildred Scott or Millie Viehweg keeping things going in the kitchen, or a couple of fellows like Harold Larson and Harry Graber having a party every Saturday night washing dishes while their wives, Helen and Addie, took care of the coffee.

A local top-flight businessman, Lloyd Reaves, a warm friend of Del Greenlee's, heard about all this and became our unexpected ally at a time of great financial need. He negotiated a loan with a bank and helped us raise a hefty down payment—$16,000. So that at the end of the first year The Firehouse Corporation became the proud, grateful owners of that old fire station for $46,000. How can you get that paid off with coffee? Yet that's exactly what's been happening.

This all started with Lloyd's moving across the aisle on a plane coming home from Chicago and asking, "Say, by the way, how's that coffee-drinking place coming along?" I gave him a casual, off-the-cuff answer, "Well, there's nothing now that a little money wouldn't solve." That was all Lloyd needed and he was off and running.

It was Maureen Knight who emerged as the faithful, gifted director of the place. We would never have made it without her! The Firehouse became her passion and joy and burden in a very special way!

Over the years Maureen had done all the worthwhile, good things in the church—the Women's Mission Society, the Sunday school, the college department—the whole works. And then her beloved Bill was killed in one of those senseless automobile accidents! He was the state executive in the credit union movement and was on his way home from a legislative meeting in Pierre. With no warning an old farm truck had limped out on the highway directly in front of him. Two hours later Bill was dead in a Mitchell hospital, and Maureen had to pick up the pieces and go on.

As if that weren't enough, three and a half years later Maureen's daughter, Sally, died one morning with an extreme attack of asthma. Her heart simply gave out. It was Doctor Bob who called me— one of those awful phone calls that always seem to come early in the morning—with the shocking word that Sally was gone, asking if I could stop by and visit with Phil a bit and then go over and give Maureen the word. You wonder at a time like that why in the world you ever went into the ministry.

So Maureen began to cast about for a mission for her life— something costly and exhilarating that she could throw herself into with everything she had. She found it at 22nd and Minnesota. It started with that casual coffee making and ended with a passionate concern for the whole venture. Somehow Maureen and The Firehouse "fit." For six years of its life she mothered it, nurtured it, and kept it moving. In a strange, beautiful way she became the friend and confidante to more misfits, outcasts, and mixed up people than any other grandmother in town. She was like a "bridge over troubled water."

You could best catch this glow and burden for The Firehouse in Maureen's life on Wednesday mornings when she was there alone checking things out. This had to be done between the Sunday night closing and the Wednesday night opening. So Wednesday became her cleanup and order day. And in many ways her "renewal" day. It was like catching her breath again before another five-night run.

From the day we opened there were the people who kept showing up, in the midst of the fun, with their hurts like open, gaping wounds. The widow who walked out from downtown, a dishwasher at the Cataract Hotel. She had no money for coffee, but someone took care of that. She had heard it was a friendly place, and she was so lonely. At her insistence she joined us for a while as a kitchen worker.

Or the young man who was about to ship out for Vietnam, scared and baffled by it all. He came every night for a week, and then wept the last night and asked us to pray for him.

Roxie Lee, now so much a part of The Firehouse, first came to us as a fresh, eager junior high kid, hanging around almost constantly, getting in the way. She was one of those "Why daddy?" kind of people. But then she began to win her spurs as a waitress. And finally decided to attend Sioux Falls College, rather than S.D. State, so she could be near The Firehouse. She's been with us ever since, kindling a lot of fires.

And Lewie Rose, who claims The Firehouse saved his sanity. He came night after night just to be among friends after his son, a brilliant medical school student, was electrocuted before Lewie's eyes cleaning one of our city swimming pools. After his second marriage Lewie threw a hilarious wedding reception at The Firehouse. Every few minutes he would stand up and shout, "I want you to meet my new bride, and the treats are on me!"

Or there is Don Harriman, a big bulk of a man, friendly and open like a St. Bernard. You can almost feel his tail wagging. He started splitting wood for our fireplace and shoveling the walk in winter, and then began to write his own kind of poetry and every once in a while would play his little harp and sing those soft, gentle songs of his. Don says, "This is my second home."

So many people
brought things
for The Firehouse—
all kinds of pots and
jars for the shelves
in the front window.
And Ray Swift brought
his gift—
a hand-carved panel
for the front door.

Don Harriman, friendly and
open like a St. Bernard,
started splitting wood for our
fireplace, and then began to
write his own kind of poetry.

It was Maureen Knight who emerged as the faithful, gifted director of The Firehouse. We would never have made it without her. And then Kenney showed up. How wonderfully God had been preparing him right under our noses to take charge of The Firehouse.

For Carole Boling, "Bo" as everyone called her, The Firehouse was a place of total rebirth. She had come around bitter and resentful, fed up with the institutional church, and wondering about life itself. But Maureen and Gloria and the Bashams were her special buddies. So she got drawn into the dream, and wound up doing all kinds of things, whatever anyone asked her—helping with the cleanup, making coffee, running errands, and finally becoming a hostess. I wonder if "Bo" ever realized how much the love and hope that seeped into her life showed in her face—shining with a new joy. She was saved by The Firehouse and has carried that life into many other ventures.

The list goes on and on—a beautiful gang of people, with names still being added.

But there is another chapter. It was almost as if that carefree joy slipped out the back door while trouble walked in the front! It didn't happen any certain afternoon of any certain week. It was a more gradual, subtle thing. We began to see less and less of our old church friends, with whom we felt so comfortable, as a new breed began to move in. They were much younger—strangers, who filled the place with noise and insolence and demands.

No one invited them. They just came. They baffled and threatened us because we didn't know how to handle them. They seemed to move in herds and were as suspicious and uptight about us as we were about them. Many of them insisted on getting ice water and toothpicks. And they consumed sugar by the bowl full, but refused to buy any coffee.

Then the rumors about drugs began to fly—and our people began to insist periodically they could smell that sweet aroma of marijuana. For a while we had quite a rash of self-made drug experts. So we had our first conference with the police, and they agreed to drop in from time to time as our friends.

But no question about it, we were into the drug culture! And at times it seemed we were about to be taken over by something dark and sinister and demonic. A couple of Saturday nights there were fist fights. This was a far deeper matter than just trying to keep some semblance of order. We would never be able to quiet things down by writing a few new rules. We were caught in the midst of a life-and-death spiritual struggle. All our strategy meetings became frustrating, heavy affairs with the smell of failure about them.

Some of our people who had been with us from the start simply told us in love, "I didn't bargain for this. I've had it. I can't go on." That eager commitment we had at the beginning had worn thin and it seemed like the living center was being dissipated and coming apart. Even closing up three or four times to regroup didn't change things much.

Yet every time we seriously faced the possibility of saying, "Our mission is complete; we're going out of business," there were a stubborn few who dug in and insisted that this was no time to quit. Not only the ones like Roxie, Don, or Bev Weiss, but Darrell Jurrens, a heavy equipment operator for the city, who had joined us as a host on Friday nights. Not the orthodox churchy kind, but a committed gutsy type, he laid it on the line. "Why do Christians always want to run for the hills when the going gets rough?"

And Maureen. She had every reason to want to close up shop and go home. Here she was trying to ride herd on a bunch of kids that were almost as alien to her as visitors from another planet. Yet she had an amazing feel for them, and somehow they knew she was playing for keeps. Many of them had cried out to her, "Where do we go if you close The Firehouse?" Somehow she knew that behind their swagger and noise and rudeness were scared little kids looking for a better deal. And she kept saying over and over again, "I believe Christ has put us here! And we ought to stay."

So we took another look at the kids and began to hear and see something new. Sure, they were scared. Many of them had been so hurt they found it next to impossible to let any of their defenses down. So many of them insisted, "This is almost like home to me—" which made us wonder what they had going for them there. Some of them even said, "Why don't you give us a chance to work here. Let us be waiters and waitresses." And when we said, "Well, why not give it a try," that's when we began to sense a shift.

All this pushed us to examine our own commitment. Maybe our earlier talk about Christ being present among us in a rather vague, incognito way had been a copout. An excuse to keep him hidden under some table assuming we could bring him out whenever the occasion seemed right, saying, "You see, this really is a Jesus place." And now he was laying it on us that he really had to be Lord of this place—or we had better give up pretending it was Christian.

If he had moved among the lepers and the blind and the outcasts of his day, finally dying between a couple of thieves on what was little more than a garbage pile, certainly he could handle The Firehouse if we would give him a chance. This whole struggle clarified the issue once again, and we declared it quite simply, "This is his place." We laid some Reachout versions of the New Testament on the tables, started a Bible study one night a week in the upper room, and brought in some Christian singing groups and encouraged them to "let it all hang out." Let the chips fall where they may.

In the midst of this a big, beautiful guy began to show up, looking things over, checking things out, testing it. Strong and gentle, with heavy black hair and penetrating blue eyes, Kenney was hard to forget, once you met him.

Kenney knew all about booze. He had come from that kind of a home. Even now his father was in a nursing home out in the western part of the state with a wet brain. Kenney had taken to the stuff early and by his late teens knew he was an alcoholic.

And drugs. He had gone the whole route, all the way to heroin. He had spent time at Yankton and on the psych ward at McKennan hoping to find a cure. And had ended up carrying the stuff from Minneapolis to Sioux Falls, hoping to pick up a few bucks.

Little wonder he was so full of suspicion and anger. So much of his life had been a failure. An aunt in California had rejected him when she discovered there wasn't any money in it for her in caring for him. That was when he was eleven. He had blown it at Lincoln High and in a variety of foster homes. Friends dropped him because he was bad medicine. He couldn't even make it when he tried to end it all with barbiturates.

But one person stubbornly refused to give up on him. Teri Williams, who kept saying, "I just know there's something good in Kenney and one of these days it's going to come out. You just wait and see!" Bill Milliken calls it "tough love"! [2] There must be some kind of special place in heaven for these kinds of believers.

Teri was right. Because some place along the line something clicked for Kenney—a key was turned. A soft, tender look began stealing into his face. It was beautiful. "But to all who did receive him," says the Apostle John, "to those who have yielded him their allegiance, he gave the right to become children of God." [3] That's what happened! Kenney had become a child of God. He had come into a new family. And he says that wondrous, strange miracle would never have taken place had it not been for those who knew the worst about him but never gave up on him.

While all this was taking place, Kenney was showing up at The Firehouse more and more, opening up a little, becoming a part of things in a shy, unobtrusive way. First as a waiter, then a host.

He knew all about these kids with their fears and hangups. Some of them he had had very intimate dealings with under other circumstances. So he understood the purpose and strategy of The Firehouse as few others—especially for his friends and all the others like them. And the urgency and intensity of that understanding grew on him.

Until one day Kenney showed up at my office. A bit nervous— after all this was his first visit to a pastor's study voluntarily—but also eagerly, like a child with a big secret. Then out it came, "I've been doing a lot of thinking. You know what The Firehouse has come to mean to me. I really believe that God wants me to work there more and more. And it may seem like a crazy thing, but I feel he wants me to be in charge of things."

It almost took my breath away. It was almost as if I knew he would make that speech before it came tumbling out. And yet that thought hadn't even crossed my mind until he showed up at the door. How wonderfully God had been preparing Kenney right under our noses without our being aware of a thing.

And what timing! For Maureen had come to feel more and more that she had fulfilled her mission, that someone else ought to take over now. A beautiful, newly married couple, Tom and Teri Hildebrand, had seen us through a brief interim. And now here came Kenney! And every place we turned, the offer of himself was confirmed—from the workers to the newly formed Firehouse Committee of the board of deacons. So after almost seven years we are getting our second wind and beginning a new chapter.

It still "doesn't make sense," but still they come—the lonely and the angry and the seeking, as well as those just out for a good time. Percy over there at the table by the wall, Beth serving as a waitress, or Gene behind the cash register with all the others. Somehow they know they're near the fire—and that means light and warmth.

8.

Getting
Their Brains
Out of Hock

It was really kind of amazing Stan was there at all.
Greeting people and passing out hymnbooks and later on helping to
take up the offering. Most folks had no idea how this tall, friendly
fellow had ended up ushering in a Baptist church for the evening
service.

Well, Stan had come to us by way of The Glory House, four
years before. A buddy from prison days had told him about this
place where the food was great and you really felt at home with
no questions asked. So Stan started showing up, especially for those
evening meals. Gulping down Edith McAuley's cooking, hanging
around afterward to shoot some pool with the other men or to
watch a little TV or simply to bat the breeze. And even though he
didn't stay there, he became like an older brother to the McAuley
girls, especially Linda.

Then one cold February Sunday Stan showed up at church. To
"case the joint" as he told Joe McAuley, even though he was a
little fidgety at first. Wondering what kind of a church would ever
get into a halfway house business. But it wasn't just a one-shot
visit, because the next Sunday he was back, and the next, and the
next. Until he became a regular.

Then one morning as we were singing the last hymn he came
down a side aisle to confess Christ with no strings attached. So
determined I think he could have walked right through a stone

wall. This was so utterly unexpected it took our breath away. Our faith often isn't as great as we imagine it is.

All I could say was, "Folks, this is Stan Ruby—a special friend God has sent our way—giving himself to Christ and wanting to follow him in baptism" (I was too choked up for anything more), and then hope a few of our folks would stop by and give him some encouragement.

Well, they did. Almost the whole congregation, it seemed, lined up to greet Stan, warmly and unashamedly. Many with an embrace or a kiss. When it was all over Stan simply said, "This is the first time in my life I've ever belonged to anybody or anything." I couldn't help noticing that we were standing by the communion table!

When Stan was baptized a few weeks later it was a demonstration all over again of those words in the Epistle to the Ephesians, "Thus you are no longer aliens in a foreign land, but fellow-citizens with God's people, members of God's household." [1] Our tears—both Stan's and mine—were mingled in the baptismal waters.

Stan really knew what those words meant. His troubles had started in Wyoming when he was twelve. There had been the pain and conflict of a broken home. Stan had lashed out at society, then done a couple of stints in the reformatory, learning all kinds of new tricks. Then came a whole series of armed burglaries—forty-one altogether—and three terms in various state penitentiaries. Nine and a half dreary, frustrating, lost years.

Then finally his day of liberty came! A whole new ball game. How could he handle this freedom now when every move and decision had been watched and dictated month after month, year after year? No wonder men come out of prison overwhelmed— with sweaty hands, all shaky and nauseated! Desperately afraid they'll make some kind of a mistake that will send them back to the pen.

Somehow Stan found a small place to live and managed to get a job at Lumbermen's Supply. That's when he began showing up at the great old pink house at 220 South Williams. As he tasted of the life in that home, his defenses began to come down. Maybe it was the easygoing banter with the girls, or that good food, or those new friends who let him come and go as he wanted to.

And there were no "hookers" in it, no religious propaganda. Only a few words of thanks at mealtime. But whatever it was, this family style began to set Stan free. That was when he asked about "that church." And when he got into it he didn't sit on the sidelines. He became a part of a small Bible study group, went out on a couple of lay witness teams, got on The Firehouse team as a host. And finally became so much a part of the establishment that he got on that ushering crew. And the door through which he came was the great, old pink house on Williams Avenue.

It's a wild, almost unreal story—how that house came to be. I'm not sure anyone can quite swallow it, and it's certain to make the rehabilitation professionals shudder. But it's part of what God has been doing with us. Some more of that open agenda business.

It started in one of our membership classes. We had come to the last session when we always speak about what "this church expects of you if you decide to come in with us." I was trying to stress the urgency of Christian people getting out "where the action is." To illustrate this I spoke a bit about The Firehouse, where we had been having the time of our lives for about a year.

And then I tossed out one of those top-of-the-head suggestions: "There are a lot of other places where church people are needed. Like giving a hand to the men coming out of the state penitentiary. Someone really ought to get a halfway house going. There's no sense for men to come out and fumble around alone against terrific odds, then make a mistake—write a bad check or get another DWI charge or into some petty thievery—and end up back in the pen again. That's ridiculous! There ought to be some place for them to get their bearings."

Talk about an off-the-cuff remark. But it was picked up. Jan Pay wanted to know, "What's a halfway house?" Well, leave it to an amateur to answer. So I plunged on. After all, I had read a little and heard a thing or two. "A halfway house is really a home, not a treatment center, for people coming out of some kind of institutional life. Long on good food and family atmosphere and love. Mostly a place of hope!" That was the best I could do.

There was a bit more discussion. "How many men 'on the hill' are repeaters?" The answer is 67 percent. "It would be a great thing to stop that kind of vicious treadmill, wouldn't it?" "After all, 'they' are someone's son or husband or brother." Then the class was

dismissed and we went our separate ways. And that was the end
of that.

But not for Jan Pay! Two days later she called and simply declared, "I've got your house." I knew she must be kidding. "What
house?" "Why, that halfway house you were talking about in the
class." She sounded hurt. "I went out and rented this beautiful old
house on the edge of town. But only for two months. Then we'll
know if we want it." I knew then she wasn't kidding, and a sinking
feeling came over me. I could only say to myself, "This poor, confused woman. She's got enough problems of her own without getting into this."

I tried to stall, "You've what!" So she repeated, a bit irritated,
"I've rented this house. I've been admiring it for a year, and it's
just perfect for what you were talking about." All I could think
was, "Why can't I ever keep my big mouth shut?" but I answered,
"We can't go out and take on a major project like this just because
you like some house." But she came at me again, "But you said this
is something we ought to be doing." I tried to crawl out as best
I could, "Jan, you can't always believe what we preachers say.
We're always sounding off on something."

Even with that feeble attempt at humor she wasn't about to give
up until I finally agreed to go out and at least take a look at this
house. A few days later she called, "Have you been out yet to see
'the' house?" "No, but I'll call you when I can shake loose." This
Jan could really hang on to something when it grabbed her. Two
and a half weeks after her first phone call, when I knew she wasn't
going to forget, I gave her a ring and three of us from the church
met her at the house.

I had to admit grudgingly it was quite something. Like the house
of seven gables—huge and pink, standing out like a fortress on the
west edge of town. And great rooms finished with lovely old wood!
From Sweden, no less! Amazing! The house had been moved out
some years before by Brandt, an old house-mover who had become
a legend around town. It had been used for all kinds of things, even
a Pentecostal church group. Maybe Jan was right! I had never
expected anything like this at all! The whole house had a warm,
inviting feeling.

But then I tried to pull back before I got carried away too far, and said, half-jokingly, "Well, it's a great place, Jan. And you'd better enjoy it while you can. Because by the time we get some of our church people out here to hear about this wild scheme that'll take care of things. But at least we can give it a try and see what happens."

So over the next couple of weeks three hastily called, ad-hoc groups gathered at 220 South Williams. About ninety people altogether—dreamers and realists once again. After giving the big house the once-over, with a lot of "oh's" and "ah's," we gathered each time for coffee and cookies which Jan had been more than eager to handle, and then spilled out the wild dream of turning this place into a halfway house. And waited for the negative reaction, which didn't come! That was the big surprise. Instead it was, "How many men could we take care of?" or "Can't you just see a big family sitting down in there to eat?" or even "When do we get underway?"

An unexpected go-ahead seemed to come when the second group met. It was a day heavy with grief—the day of Martin Luther King's assassination. There was no way we could shake the pain of his death. As we were about to leave, almost absent-mindedly Jan Pay sat down at the old battered piano, left by that Pentecostal group, and began to play in a rather syncopated style,

Mine eyes have seen the glory of the coming of the Lord,
He is trampling out the vintage where the grapes of wrath are
stored.

Before we knew what had happened everyone was gathered around the piano—twenty-five or thirty strong—singing lustily,

"Glory, glory, Hallelujah . . .
His truth is marching on!"

The release of something deep within us that needed to get out.

Going down the old stairs on our way out, someone caught me by the arm. "Well, there's only one name for this place. And that's The Glory House!" The name stuck, and so that's how we later incorporated.

Well, it was quite a day when we gathered that Sunday afternoon to make *the* decision. Everyone knew we were rushing in where angels fear to tread. But this didn't seem to hold anyone back. We would turn this great old place into a home for wounded, needy men. That's what everyone had come to say. A board was named, many of them volunteers who wanted in on the action. And task forces were named to get the old place cleaned up, to raise some money, find furniture and dishes, and find someone who would come and live here as our halfway house director. The meeting was full of open, risky talk and all kinds of beautiful hilarity. It was almost inevitable that we should end by singing once again, "Mine eyes have seen the glory of the coming of the Lord."

All this was laid before our church family at a business meeting and, bless them, they ended up confirming The Glory House as a ministry of First Baptist, giving the pastors the freedom to guide the work.

During all this the names of Joe and Edith McAuley kept running through my mind. Was it possible they might be the ones to direct the affairs of this house and make it into a home? That would take some doing. Most recently Joe had been handling a delivery route for a dry cleaning firm in Ottawa, Kansas. And what a leavening influence he had turned out to be! So many unhappy, lonely people coming to their doors to pick up the cleaning, to find little, friendly Joe with their clothes. And with that introduction he became the confidant and friend of many of these people. He had also been a moving spirit among many of the alcoholics in that town.

He and Edith had lived through all kinds of trouble—the years of Joe's alcoholism, the constant struggle to keep the wolf from the door, the shame of Joe's time in the state mental hospital. But all this had shaped and mellowed them. And best of all thrown them back again and again on the grace of our Lord.

But Joe was restless, that I knew, looking for something that might be right for him. Could that possibly be The Glory House? So we talked it over and agreed there was only one way to find out —have Joe come up if he were willing, particularly if he were willing to fly, since he was deathly afraid of planes. But we had no money. And once again it was Jan who asked if she couldn't pick up the tab. Even when we came to feel that Edith should come along, because a great hunk of this would be on her back, Jan took care of the whole thing.

This Jan was certainly turning out to be something else. She had caught a vision and wasn't going to let go of it.

How well I remember the day she had come swinging into my office—well tailored, exuding all kinds of confidence, it seemed. "A lady of breeding," as Gert Behanna would say. Could I help get her husband straightened out? she wanted to know. Not an unusual request these days. And when I asked her "Why me?" she came right back. "Your name is in the yellow pages, and I understood you are supposed to be a community leader." I wondered about that "community leader" business, but was delighted someone had found us in the yellow pages. The first time as far as I know.

But if her husband was the big problem, then why bring her sister along for moral support, and why keep those dark glasses on, and why all that nervous fidgeting with her keys?

For some reason I agreed to visit with her husband, and that turned out to be a disaster. And Jan's coming back for a "report" wasn't much better. I was surprised she seemed eager to come back again.

That was when her defenses came tumbling down. She had barely gotten through the door before she slumped into a chair and finally pulled off those dark glasses. Then she reached into her handbag, yanked out an odd little green rubbery character, plopped it on my desk, and quietly sobbed, "That's me!" What a strange thing to do. Until I noticed the name on the little fellow's neck— "Hopeless." We simply sat there for a couple of long minutes, the room full of her pain. Finally all I could say was, "Jan, welcome to the club. That's where we all start. I guess I knew you felt hopeless the first time you came. But believe me, that's not the last word." And that was the start of her pilgrimage.

Months later—after falling down and getting up half a dozen times—the miracle started happening. But what a struggle!

How does a strong, self-willed woman like Jan turn it all over to the only One who can carry the whole load? Particularly if it's been drilled into you ever since childhood that the strong ones stand on their own two feet? It wasn't just the booze and the pills or those fears and guilt, but that awful pride and self-sufficiency. How can you be sure you can trust anyone? But then one day she gave it all to God. That was when she brought another little doll to the office. This time the word "Hope" was sewed on the front. And that tells the story.

Now she was released to share some of that fierce determination and beautiful generosity with any who might come her way—which had turned out to be an amazing collection of friends. Verla, carrying her unborn child and reaching out so desperately for love. I thought Jan might tear up both city hall and our church finding housing and support for her. And Bev Weiss, longing for a friend who would not fail her. Hardly able to believe that Jan would be interested in her after that first visit. After all, they were so far apart socially. But Jan stuck by her all the way.

And there were many others. Even her own daughter, Lollie, in a time of despair and confusion. And a great old stalwart churchman like Jay B. Allen, our moderator emeritus. They became fast friends. Jan became the mother hen for a beautiful conglomeration of strays called the Dandelions.

And there would have been no Glory House without Jan Pay!

Well, Joe and Edith's visit turned out to be like a marriage. That wild halfway house crowd fell in love with the two of them and they responded in the same way. Once again we sang the "Battle Hymn" which by now had become our unofficial theme song, and sent them home to think it over.

Which didn't take very long, because they had barely gotten home—it was Monday during supper—when the phone rang. It was Joe and Edith, like a couple of excited kids. "Well, it looks like this is something we're supposed to try. We're awfully scared, but this seems to be what God has been getting us ready for. So we're going to pull up our roots, bring the three girls, and come." It was as simple as that! Now we had a director!

In the meantime our crews had gone to work trying to make things shipshape. Harold Wingler did so well at scrounging the furniture that he became the first board chairman. Some reward! Jack Holt brought in the kitchenware and the dishes. Mary Oines and Fran Stewart and Jan gave the place a cleaning from top to bottom. LeRoy Day and Les Hash drew up some simple procedures.

No alcohol in the house. No gambling. No women on the second floor. 1:00 A.M. curfew. And any man who worked would pay $25 a week. Otherwise, we'd carry him.

Even the plumbers got together—labor and management—and we ended up with a shower and a new bathroom. A gift! This meant we could handle five men fairly comfortably.

Bob Wangsness and Oliver Clark rented a truck and went down to Kansas to pick up the McAuleys' earthly goods—slim pickings after all these years. The report of that trip is good for a lot of belly laughs any time it's rehearsed. And it keeps getting better with age!

But about the time we thought we were all set, our troubles began to surface. Our neighbors ganged up on us to block our request for a special zoning permit. We had assumed this was a mere formality—but not so! Rumors and fears began to take over: "Our daughters will be raped." "Think of what will happen to our land values." "Our neighborhood will be full of sex deviates and murderers and thieves." "Why don't the rich people let something like this come into their neighborhood?" Some of us tried to meet with these folks to talk things over, but we were almost shouted down.

Finally the day came for the special hearing on the zoning permit, before the City Commission. The big room was packed and tense. I was learning a thing or two about life in the public sector. First the mayor asked if there were any objections to a permit for a halfway house at 220 South Williams. One of the "protesters" stepped forward with a petition, and proceeded in rather strong language to speak about "bringing criminals into our neighborhood who will be dangerous for our children to be around" and "property values going down" and "weren't there other places in town where this could be done just as well?" And then he concluded by giving the mayor a sheaf of papers "signed by more than four hundred people in our neighborhood who simply aren't going to let something like this happen." I remember thinking, "How fitting. He's wearing a black suit, even though he looks out of place in it. Like a mortician presiding over the death of a beautiful dream."

Then came our chance. Trying to explain what we were about. Why this halfway house? How do you break the endless "in-and-out" routine of the repeater in prison unless something like this is tried? Yes, a home for five men is small with almost four hundred men in the prison. But "it is better to light a candle than. . . ." And so The Glory House. Not a treatment center. But a home. "And let's not forget that every man locked up is someone's son or brother or husband." And, "Yes, we are amateurs, but since when does that exclude us from giving it a try?"

But in spite of all that there was a spirit of stubborn resistance in the air. Then, before closing our side of the argument, I introduced Joe and Edith to the mayor and the others. It was a final, somewhat hopeless, gesture. "These are the folks we had hoped might run this house and be friends to any men who might come our way." I never expected that Joe would ask if he could say a few words.

But he did, and it turned out to be some witness—quiet and intense and terribly honest. About his old, desperate life of alcoholism. How Edith had never left him, loving him all the time. Then how God had changed his life "on the river bank while I was fishing." And what it had been like to live without alcohol, with new friends and new hope. And while he had done a lot of different things to keep body and soul together, he had always dreamt that some day he might work with men in a halfway house. "We just want a chance to try something like this."

Then he introduced Edith—the room was now hushed and people were straining to hear every word, almost holding their breath. And then, "These are my three daughters—Kathy, who is fourteen, and Donna, who is thirteen, and Lindy, who is ten. And, Mr. Mayor, I guess if anyone's daughters is going to be raped, they'll be mine!" Then he sat down!

There was a long pause and then Mayor Schirmer spoke quietly, "In my judgment this Glory House is something really needed in our city. I believe the matter has been thoroughly discussed, and I now will ask for a vote on the question. I'm voting in favor of the request."

Then Commissioner McCart spoke up. "My mother lives out there near that house and I know the neighborhood real well." "Oh, oh," I thought, "here it goes." But he went on, "So I asked her what she thought about this halfway house business. And she said she thought it was a great idea, so I'm joining the Mayor in voting for this special permit." Then Commissioner Witte voted affirmatively. And that did it! Talk about the Holy Spirit in the marketplace! We could only praise God.

Incidentally, since then our neighbors have become our friends and affirmed us again and again! Even joining in on some of our anniversary celebrations.

So we opened up the big house and let our friends come to see what we were trying to do—and meet the McAuleys. Amid all the excitement we took an offering in a big old coffeemaker that someone had painted orange.

And then waited! Now that everything was really clean and shiny, how were we going to get ourselves some business? Find a man or two at least to find out if this was all going to work. For a month that was our "in" joke. Then our first "customer" showed up. Not at all as we had planned. You might have guessed that. He came in the middle of the night, quite drunk and miserable.

That's when our phone rang. It was Joe all excited. "Our first man just came." "But why call me at this time of the morning—2:00 or whenever it is?" "Well," Joe said, "he's drunk and you know about those rules we drew up." That was right—"No whiskey in the house."

All I could do was throw the ball back to Joe. "What do you think we ought to do?" "Give him some coffee and put him to bed and decide in the morning what we're going to do." What else could I do but agree and stumble back to bed.

In the morning we decided to "keep" Gene, even though he hadn't come the way we had planned it—sober and respectable in the middle of the day.

He had done almost ten years in the pen for one car theft after another. So when he finally was released he did a very smart thing —bought an old jalopy with most of his hard-earned prison savings. And helped answer that part of our Lord's prayer, "And do not bring us to the test, but save us from the evil one." [2]

But that called for a modest celebration—a drink or two at the Rainbow Bar. One thing led to another and next Gene was setting up drinks for everyone in the place. A "good time Charlie" after all those dreary, lonely months in prison. In the spirit of the celebration Gene left his wallet on the bar—and someone "cleaned" him. That was when he left, disgusted and fed up with it all, heading for Pierre, hoping to see his mother for the first time in eleven years.

But seven or eight miles west of town one of those aging tires

Stan Ruby,
who now works
in a lumberyard,
came to us by way of
The Glory House.

It was Jan Pay who was
responsible for our get-
ting The Glory House
—huge and pink, stand-
ing out like a fortress
on the west edge of
town. "I've got your
halfway house," she
told us.

Edith and Joe McAuley
had lived through
all kinds of trouble.
In it all Edith had never
left him, loving him
all the time.

Marvin Menholt (left) has nursed Sunrise manufacturing along, and now
truck after truck rolls out loaded with rafters for mobile homes, making
the difference between staying open and closing for The Glory House.

gave out. And there was a dog who took off after Gene and then an
angry farmer who ended up calling the sheriff's office. The deputy
who answered the call had been a guard at the penitentiary during
part of Gene's stay there. He remembered Gene and insisted he
couldn't put him, sick as he was, back in jail without booking him.
"You're too good a man to go through all that again, Gene," was
all he would say. But he vaguely remembered having heard about
a halfway house. "Seems to me I read about it in the paper. Maybe
they'd take you." And we did. That is how Gene Peters ended up
at 220 South Williams.

After a visit home—the deacons' fund helped buy a used tire
and some gas—Gene came back and found a job. And, wonder of
wonders, it was with a top-flight car dealer, Henry Billion, who has
given many a man a chance at a new start. It's a standing joke
around The Glory House how Gene came in one night excitedly
waving a key. "Look at this. There must be a million dollars worth
of cars in that place. And I've got the key!" Quite a spot for an old
car thief!

But Gene made good. After six months at The Glory House he
took off on his own. Now he's with the Highway Department and
happily married to Robin with a lovely three-year-old son. If you
were to drop by our Youth Room at the church on a Friday night
about seven o'clock, you'd find Gene with twelve or thirteen boys
around the tables in Scout uniforms—the new, enthusiastic Scout-
master of rejuvenated Troop 23.

Gene was the first of 121 men to come our way in these six years
of doing business. All kinds of them—salesmen, schoolteachers,
mechanics, carpenters. Many of them greatly gifted, all of them
hoping for some kind of a chance. But some of them not willing
to give up the old game of conning. And we've sadly watched those
men move back into the shadows to play the same old games again.
Like Ben, who filled his dresser drawer with marijuana, arguing
that someone else was trying to frame him.

They've come in all colors—red, white, and black. Staying for
varying periods of time—one man for only two days and Paul Dor-
wart for fourteen months. With the help of Vocational Rehabilitation Paul finished his accounting work at Augustana College and
went on to pass his C.P.A. exam. He is now a private accountant in
Arizona after doing a stint with the Air Force. Before it was all

over we were calling him "Pope Paul" at our Friday morning men's Bible group. Now he calls us every once in a while from Arizona to see if we're still able to get along without him.

One of our "alums" is a city electrical inspector in a neighboring city, another is an aide in a hospital, and another is farming near here. Altogether we know where at least thirty-one or thirty-two of these men are. Far more a part of the answer than of the problem.

"How many successes?" we are often asked. Well, how do you measure that? As Joe says, "We don't have no failures, because that's where we start."

But is any act of love lost? When will some memory—one of Edith's meals or the kidding of one of the girls or a Christmas celebration—come to mind and bring a man up short? Like the crowing of a cock. And be a call to come home. So how can we mark any man down finally as a failure?

We have often spoken about Larry Baulch coming to give us some encouragement and guidance at the start. He had all the credentials. His book, *Return to the World*,[3] tells the story—the bitterness and crime of his early years and eventually his three stints in San Quentin. Then getting into a Yokefellow group and the door beginning to swing open. So Larry got into the business of rehabilitating all kinds of men coming out of prison life.

His message for us "nice" square people, so eager to help others, was, "It's not what you'll do for them. It's what these men will do for you! Listen to them and learn from them." How right he was. For they have constantly shaken us up, angered us, stretched us, and always kept us open. They have refused to let us play games, and often touched us to the quick with their unexpected streaks of tenderness and gratitude. So many of them have come to us hurt and lonely and defensive, eagerly grasping at every scrap of love coming their way. How could we be around this without becoming a bit more human?

Our constant, nagging problem at The Glory House has been money—simply keeping our heads above water—even though it has cost us only about a thousand dollars a month to keep things going, which is a bargain as halfway houses go. What a great debt we owe Ed Oines, a sharp, concerned businessman, who has watched those books like a hawk. And before him it was Ralph Maples.

And we've lived with cliff-hangers. Early in the game we were behind $253 with no money in the bank—and Christmas was on us! About this time, at Rotary Club one Monday I happened to sit next to John Foss, pastor of our neighboring First Presbyterian Church. As the meal and program were ending, John leaned across the table and said quite casually, "By the way, we had some money left over in our Mission Fund and our deacons voted a couple of nights ago to give $260 to the halfway house. How do I make out the check?" I could only gulp and ask, "How much did you say, John?" He might have wondered about my hearing, but he didn't let on—only repeated, "$260." And I could only thank him while I prayed under my breath, "Thanks, Lord. You gave us $7 more than we needed."

We never could have made it without miracles like that. Or friends who have a beautiful way of coming through just in the nick of time in response to one of our pleas. Or the regular support from the Presbyterians and the Methodists and the Lutherans. And Joe picking up a bit of help here and there as he's moved around telling the story. But that's still a hit and miss way of doing it.

Then one day Lloyd Reaves got into the act. Not so much by human design, I'm convinced, as by divine guidance. And not across the aisle of a plane this time. His wife, Char, had come home from a P.E.O. meeting and reported that her group had voted to give $25 to help The Glory House. "What for?" Lloyd asked. "Groceries," she replied. "But that won't buy a lot of groceries." "Oh, but it was to help with a bill." "Well, how much is that?" "I think they said about $1600." "Wha-a-a-t?" was all Lloyd could say.

But it set him thinking. There ought to be some better way to finance that place than in this sporadic, hand-to-mouth way. So this was all on him when he showed up at a small fund-raising luncheon at the home a few days later, which I chalked off pretty much as a failure—hardly anyone we expected came and it all seemed pretty flat and tasteless. But Lloyd heard the story and met Joe. And the grocery bill got taken care of and a dream was born.

A few days later he shared the dream over coffee. Why not get some kind of small manufacturing place going where the men in the house could be put to work? That would mean a guarantee of steady employment for them and at least $25 a week from each man working. And eventually the profits, if there were any, could go to The Glory House.

There was no way this could be dismissed as some "fly-by-night" scheme. Because the man talking this way was running an extremely successful business and was known as the kind who could put dreams in overalls and get things going.

But what kind of a business? Well, it could be plastic lures. Joe would like that because he's a fishing nut. Or maybe furniture, or even plastic all-weather trellises. And there we left it—except we agreed to get together again if the right man surfaced who could take over this kind of a wild dream and make it go.

For days I wondered if there were anyone who could run a place like that. And a couple of names came to mind. Then one day Marvin Menholt showed up on our breezeway coming by for his weekly half-glass of milk—a substitute for his old boozing days and an "in" joke between him and Ruth. All of a sudden it hit me, "This is your man. He's a strong takeover type with all kinds of moxie and experience." At one time or another he had managed a couple of lumberyards, handled all kinds of heavy road equipment, worked for the city Park Department, and even been with a landscaping company.

But alcohol had almost finished all that—and Marvin too. After years of fierce wrestling with his awful feelings of inferiority and the bottle, Marvin had come to see me at the insistence of a physician. We first met at Kirk's West, a restaurant on the edge of town. Better there than in a church office. Even then he came in twenty minutes late—red-faced and extremely nervous.

And so another intensive struggle began. There were times of beautiful, childlike sobriety and others of sadistic, angry drinking. Marvin could gulp it down like few men I have known—raw with no mixer at all. I have no idea how many times he had been in and out of one hospital or treatment center after another. He had even spent a short time at The Glory House.

But now he had a new Ally and Power—and little by little he was winning the battle. As the people in the church came to know Marvin, they loved him and affirmed him and drew him into things. We have had many laughs about Marvin showing up to do some yard work for us during his first stretch of sobriety, wearing heavy winter underwear on a warm Monday in May because he had no other clothes. Or going to the home concert of the Sioux Falls College choir sitting between Ruth and me, so shaky we wondered if he'd make it. Stuck between a pastor and his wife trying to listen to classical church music. What a predicament to get into.

But there was a lot of power in Marvin. Maybe what he needed to put it all together was a hefty, tough challenge like this dream. So when he and Lloyd got together and began to talk things over, "Sunrise Manufacturing" was born.

A big old warehouse on North Cliff was leased from Tom Costello. And before Christmas that year Marvin and three of the Glory House men had the place all cleaned up and were getting the jigs ready. At first it was going to be trellises! But people aren't thinking about flowers in January—at least not in South Dakota. We've still got some left we're trying to market—more than two years later.

But we hit our stride when the men began to make rafters for mobile homes. At least there was a market for them. So they went to work, with Marvin running the show and Amos and Del and Bob from The Glory House—an unlikely crew, but eager. The equipment was primitive to say the least—some jigs and lumber, some glue and staples, and, oh yes, a saw.

Lloyd and Marvin had figured things out right on the button— it would take 204 rafters a day to break even. The first day the best that crew could do was 38. All Amos could say was, "We'll never make it!" But twelve days later Marvin called shortly before four o'clock like a kid with a new toy. "We've just finished our 203rd rafter." All I could say was, "Well, let's keep the celebration down to coffee and I'll be right over!"

Now two years later, truck after truck rolls out loaded with tough, resilient rafters—U.L. and state inspected and approved— on their way to mobile home plants in Missouri, Nebraska, and South Dakota. They've been put together by men no self-respecting employment agency would give a second thought, some giving it a try on "work release" from the penitentiary, or just home from alcoholic treatment at Yankton or the V.A. Hospital or River Park, with the men at The Glory House getting first chance. Some of the men are so shaky they can hardly hold the tools, but they are struggling to find dignity and a new beginning.

They're treated like men who will deliver—not babied along. A full day's work—8:30 to 4:30—minimum wage and some piece work incentive. And this ragged battalion has come through with flying colors. There isn't a place in town with better morale or production record. It's the best illustration of private initiative, business know-how, and compassion joined in a common cause I know anything about.

Marvin has nursed Sunrise along. Pushing when he had to, giving a man a slap on the back when he needed it, talking to him like a dutch uncle when he had that coming, and laying a man off now and then if he couldn't pull the load. Pulling off a miracle with men and work in that order.

In fact things have moved along so well that in the last few months we've gotten into making draperies for mobile homes with four or five women and a half dozen sewing machines.

Here and there quiet reminders of hope have begun to show up at Sunrise. Like the "Serenity Prayer" right out in plain sight in Marvin's office. "Lord, grant me the serenity to accept the things I cannot change, the courage to change the things I can, and the wisdom to know the difference."

Then it was the "24-Hour Book," a gutsy little spiritual guide for men trying to work the A.A. program. The men agreed among themselves to come a few minutes early each morning so they could start things off with this. Then little round smiling faces began showing up here and there on the walls with the word "Sunshine."

The first year of operation the men at the halfway house brought home $4721.52 at their $25 a week, twice as much as the year before. And gifts totaling $1650 came to The Glory House from Sunrise—the difference between staying open and closing.

Just now the Sunrise Board has voted to pick up the total salary of the Director of The Glory House. Not bad for a beginning! "A way that starts from faith and ends in faith," [4] the Apostle Paul said. How true! From a membership class to The Glory House, and from a fund-raising luncheon to Sunrise Manufacturing! How wondrously God has been in it all!

In the last few months we've been taking a long hard look at our ministry in the big pink house. That faithful, long-suffering board with Gene Pierce as chairman and Ed Oines as treasurer. Are we doing all we can for the men? Should we be moving to a new location? Who will succeed Joe and Edith when they have to step aside? In the middle of one of those sessions, Joe put it about as well as I've ever heard it. "We're here to help a man get his brains out of hock, and that's why we'll always be here. Why, it takes at least six months of freedom for a man to get his brains out of hock."

Jesus said it another way right at the start of his ministry. "He has anointed me . . . to proclaim release for prisoners." [5] And that's the business he's gotten us into.

9.

Meanwhile,
Back at
22nd and Covell

Back at 22nd and Covell is where we do our business, in a beautiful, colonial-style building that stands out over the neighborhood like a graceful watchman. Well-manicured lawns and a carefully laid-out parking lot surround it, and chimes in the tower call people to worship three times every Sunday and to prayer every Wednesday night. Our neighbors must wonder about all those cars that constantly come and go for every kind of meeting you can imagine.

Here we live with all those institutional questions. "Will there be enough money to fix the boiler or pay for the choir supper?" "Will someone make the announcement that the Paint and Hammer Circle has changed its time of meeting?" "Can the Philathea Class use the parlor next Thursday for their monthly meeting?" "Will you, Vic, take the hospital calling on Monday?" "Byron, we need your letter for the *Times* by 1:00." "Did anyone find the brown hat that was left here last Sunday?" "Do we have a teacher for the fourth grade class?" On and on it goes week after week. Sometimes we hardly have time to pray.

The average churchgoer feels so much better about his church when the phone is answered promptly and pleasantly by someone who seems to know what's going on, and the temperature in the building is right, and the announcements don't get goofed up. And he wants a pastor around—which means in the building—

when he calls. "After all," he may say, "look what we're paying them."

There's a subtle, relentless pressure in all this expectation. The temptation is to try nervously to keep the kind of program going that will simply keep people happy. We must keep the boat from rocking at all costs, we feel. We let all that institutional business—balancing the budget and keeping the rest rooms clean—become an end in itself, gobbling up the major chunk of our energy and time, so that we "seek first all these other things" and then expect the Kingdom of God and his righteousness to be added to us.

Then when people show up longing for a bit of time and attention and love, they are an interruption in our routine. We can barely give them a quick handshake or pat on the back or a "mini-prayer" in some corner before we hurry back to the mimeograph machine or the next committee meeting. No wonder they leave with that hurt, bewildered look in their eyes.

And the sad thing about all this is that some of the most needy, troubled people are sitting right there on the very boards and committees that are drawing up the plans to remodel the kitchen or get things organized "so that we can help people"! Untouched and frustrated! And we call this "church work."

If this is true, then what happens when a church like ours—well-organized and respectable—begins to open up a little here and there. Not just the building, but in its style of life. Because the joy and ferment in the small groups and lay witness teams won't stay "out there" bottled up some place. People want to tell you about it. So it spills over into all kinds of regular church affairs.

The excitement can't be locked up in that renovated fire station at 22nd and Minnesota or in that big old pink house at 220 South Williams. It comes right into the sanctuary. Because all kinds of interesting new people, some with long hair and beards or dressed in jeans or gingham, began showing up for church affairs—even the midweek service. Some with prison records and many with drug or alcohol problems. And not only these people, but our regulars, begin to greet one another more noisily, even hugging one another right in church. And an occasional "amen" or "right on" might come forth during worship.

And every now and then something quite unexpected happens. Like Wally James, an entertainer on the Holiday Inn circuit, standing up one evening and simply blurting out, "Is there any reason why I can't be baptized with the others tonight? I've come to know Christ." Of course there wasn't! And he joined the others, making his own confession of faith in the earthy language of the entertainment world, standing there in the water.

But all this gets beyond the public meetings, right into the heart of things—even the church council. And here big questions are being asked. How we've been making decisions and electing board members and officers. Wondering if our understanding of church leadership isn't far too pragmatic. And they've even been saying, "Maybe we're paying too much attention to downtown business methods and *Robert's Rules of Order* and not enough to the New Testament."

This kind of discussion is going on right now. Exhilarating and full of promise, because it has become a serious, prayerful seeking for the mind of Christ. "Are we really willing to live under his authority? And order the life of his Body as he wills?" It's no wonder our agenda has gotten shaken up and changed.

The same kind of spirit got into a stewardship task force last fall. Before it was over everything was up for grabs, the way we'd been trying to motivate people, the kind of slogans and pledge cards we'd been using—all of it. All thirteen people ended up at the same place saying, "Why don't we really try living by faith? If our Lord is the source of everything, then what's a quarter million dollar budget to him?"

As a result no pledge cards were turned in last fall, although a couple of our people had to bring something in writing to us, or, as they said, they "just wouldn't feel right."

We simply encouraged our church family to cast out their seed in faith, even when they were certain they didn't have any—and then expect a miracle! We gave them a couple of oat seeds in a small cellophane bag as a reminder.

And now we know a beautiful miracle is unfolding. At the end of the first quarter of this year we're $10,000 ahead of a year ago.

But there are the Marthas and Andrews, the bread-and-butter Christians, who get concerned and even uptight about all this change. They wonder, "What's happening to my church?" So do I. Especially when things seem out of control—which really means my control. Sometimes I almost wish that some incident, not too grievous, would cause us to lock up the building again. Maybe that would quiet things down and it would all become more simple again. But then I know there's no way we can turn back!

Even though a few of the dissatisfied ones have left us—a couple of them saying, "It's gotten too political"—thank God the vast majority have stuck. It has been people like the Tom Harkisons, Edna Roberts, Jay B. Allen and Hilda Coon, the Jim Nelsons and the Harry Boyds—the stubbornly faithful ones—and a host of others like them, who have given the church substance and resilience in the midst of change. Certainly they have not always agreed, but they have dared believe and pray. And even affirm. Knowing that the power of God is far too explosive to be cooped up within four walls, that it must be let loose in the marketplace, and that no method or structure is ever finally sacred.

But there is no way to avoid the tension, the confrontation between the old and new. Wasn't it this way when Jesus healed the paralytic on the sabbath? His freedom and compassion upset the institutional applecart. But the Kingdom of God, this new Reality, was at hand, and no amount of murmuring about blasphemy or destroying the sabbath could hold it back.

And so the big question is always there, if one has decided to stick with the organized church. Can the necessary institutional business—the constant planning, budgeting, committeeing—be shaken loose, opened up, renewed and redirected, so that a specific congregation can become more and more a healing, liberating, reconciling community through which Christ does his ministry? Will the institution lose its life to find it for Jesus' sake? And can this happen in a place like ours without tearing it up?

Yes, I believe it can!

That stubborn conviction—that life can break forth in the middle of the establishment, that an organized suburban church can become more and more Christian—has kept me working with this one congregation now for fifteen years.

But this has been far more than "my stubborn conviction"—a personal struggle I must win to save face or come out on top. If so, I would have left long ago. No, the Lord of the Church, the One who called me here in the first place, won't let me go. This is his doing—renewing and calling forth a people "claimed by God for his own, to proclaim the triumphs of him who has called you out of darkness into his marvellous light." [1] And he's allowing me to be a part of all that he is doing to this congregation, shaking me up and even humiliating me, that in the end he may cleanse and heal me, until I come to love these people as he loves them. Teaching me what it means to live in submission to them.

Which doesn't mean that I haven't been all set to pack up and move at least a dozen times, full of angry, hurt feelings, like a pouting, uptight Elijah. Another one of "my schemes" has taken a beating or we have had a particularly bad spirit at one of our board meetings or we've been having trouble with the budget or someone has jumped on me—unjustly I've felt! And so I've gotten all set to leave. "Let them get someone else and see how well he can do with all this."

And about that time the Lord has let some beautiful miracle take place right under our noses. Without even consulting me.

Like that morning in the back of Smitty's, after our men's breakfast, when Wes Nelson gave it all to God—on his knees with the rest of us who were still there. It came from the depths. "Lord, I've tried to run my life long enough and feel I've really messed it up. Now will you come in and run it?"

But why Wes? Who would have thought he had problems? Managing a successful accounting business with his father, with a lovely family, president of the Lions Club, a great hunter and outdoor man. And so conscientious about everything he did at the church, whether it was sponsoring the senior highs or serving as a trustee.

"Then why all those inner conflicts?" he kept asking himself. That terrible sense of never being worthy of God's grace. That he had to earn his way to heaven, which meant he'd never make it! And why was he so critical of people with whom he disagreed?

Finally in quiet desperation Wes began to pray, more for himself and less for those he wanted to remake, that he might be given a new heart and a new attitude. That's when he began to be "unlocked," to love the very ones he had criticized. And that included me, because I had been on his list. Wes told me all about that one Friday morning. Said he had to. And we met each other once again in a time of beautiful reconciliation. Thank God for lay people who will level with you.

That's how we ended up on our knees in Smitty's back room.

It was a new beginning. Wes's office became a place of special help for anyone who wanted it, and he began to get a kick out of the Tuesday night calling with the other deacons.

Whenever that kind of thing has happened, I've unpacked, knowing how childish and self-centered I've been, remembering that "the One who started the good work in you will bring it to completion by the Day of Christ Jesus." [2] This is his Church, and any new life in it will be his doing, not mine.

Then I have marveled once again how these people—this congregation the Lord has given me to serve—have "hung in there" with me, not throwing me out when I've gotten pushy or impatient or self-righteous, but staying by, and even encouraging me. And what an act of faithful love that has been.

That has set me free once again. So I've been able to live with both the confines and the openness of an established church that is coming alive, to move back and forth between the faithful ones serving within the structures and the mavericks all caught up in the new things. They are one people who need each other. And I have been called to be the pastor of all of them!

Then I have been able to see again how those free-wheeling ministries begun at the edge of the institution are touching and renewing the center.

Like at a deacons' meeting not long ago. There wasn't much on the agenda, and our chairman knew we'd be on our way home very shortly. But the people had other ideas. You can't take communion out to thirty-five or so shut-ins without bringing back some kind of report. "I wish every one of you could have been with us when we took communion to Darlene Stockwell. You know she's been in that wheelchair for thirty-four years. So full of joy you can almost see her halo. Talk about being blessed!" Nor can you open The Firehouse night after night without something going on. "Have any of you met Percy? He sits over by the wall every night with a soft smile on his face. A gentle, simple guy who's just thankful he's found a new family." That's the way the comments kept coming.

Finally Del leaned over and whispered, "Well, the agenda just got shot to pieces half an hour ago." Before it was over we were drenched with laughter and tears and prayer. That could never have happened if the members had not come with some kind of expectancy. But it was Del who was wise enough to let the agenda go. That was the key to the meeting.

It hadn't always been that way. Many of us had known Del in his defensive, uncertain days, and felt the bite of his sarcasm. That was when he had resigned from the deacons in a huff. Then he and Marlys had lost a baby at birth, and passed through a heavy night of sorrow and bitterness. They had been so eager for this boy after three girls.

Not long afterward Del started showing up at the Friday morning breakfast. He seemed to let go a little, although he often was more eager for an argument than a word of love. Then his close friend and Sunday school teacher, Bob Olson, was killed in a frightful car accident in the early morning on his way to a favorite duck blind. That shook our whole congregation from stem to stern, but really tore Del up.

It was then Del threw all caution to the wind and decided to buy in. We were amazed how quickly a new tenderness started coming to him, a willingness to listen to others and even give in. He was eager, it seemed, to become a servant of the Lord, even going off to Joliet, Illinois, on a lay team with Wes Nelson on only a few hours' notice. As he put it later, "against my better judgment."

Even then, when the diaconate decided to name him chairman, I couldn't help wondering, "Why are these people doing a thing like this? Certainly there are half a dozen people better prepared for this than Del." But they understood better than I what was really taking place. And their choice was confirmed beautifully at this meeting.

The same kind of thing has been happening in a "call committee"—eleven people named by our congregation to draw up job descriptions for both a "Minister of Christian Teaching" and a "Minister with Youth." And then they must find the ones "gifted" for these ministries. An impossible task, unless these people were given an unusual spirit of wisdom and freedom.

We had gotten into this venture because of a series of thirty unstructured, free-wheeling home discussions asking about where our church is and what it ought to be doing. People held nothing back—I went to enough of them to know that—critical or positive or imaginative. They wondered about things like "Why do we keep floundering in our teaching job?" "We seem to get lots of people into our church, but what happens to them then? Where do they hook in?" "How can I grow spiritually? You know, I really need to learn something about the Bible." "With all the kids running around the church we certainly ought to be able to get a terrific youth program put together." Out of this kind of talk we arrived at twelve priorities for our life and witness. And so the call committee.

And there was nothing canned about the way these people went at it. First, they named Owen Halleen, the principal at Washington High School, their chairman, and Kim Stewart, a senior at Lincoln High School and incidentally their homecoming queen, as secretary. Owen turned out to be a special kind of gift, a perceptive and loving leader who was eager for everyone to have his say, but who also knew when to move things along. And who was not afraid to let hostilities and differences surface, convinced that in the end we would know the will of God. That's why he was free to let us stop and pray every now and then about some particular matter. I could easily understand why the kids at Washington loved and respected him.

We could never have gotten through all those profiles and references and interviews with at least a dozen people if we hadn't been honest with one another. And that's a big part of being a "community of the Spirit." Which may have been the major discovery of all those meetings.

Then one evening at the Halleen home it struck me who these people were. Jerry Adrian, a deacon and a sod farmer who had come alive on one of our lay teams; Cindy Hash, a homemaker all excited about her calling as a church school teacher; Tom Mc-Comber, chairman of our church council, who had found something very real in that Friday morning men's group; Mrs. Van Ausdall, a lovely, wise grandmother with a gift for speaking the right word at the right time. Mrs. Van had had the time of her life on the lay witness team that went to Monmouth, Illinois. A lot of people will hardly venture across town. It was that way all around the room. That's why there was so much eagerness about what could happen in the church.

Little wonder Byron Rogillio was called to be our Minister of

Christian Teaching, to leave a seminary post and become a part of the life of our congregation. Byron, who has just arrived, will not be the usual kind of technique or promotional director, which has been stock in trade for Christian Education people. He has come to be our teacher and to help equip us to teach one another as the family of God, believing there is nothing more exciting or important than the word of God coming alive among his people—in all kinds of supportive groups, especially in the family.

Then we found Dale Saxon at the end of a long list of candidates —a beautiful surprise. I've dubbed him the "Rollie Fingers" of our staff because of his lovely handlebar mustache. Dale has just begun to share his life with our young people—hundreds of them come through our doors—and their counselors, going through the pain and excitement of discovering what it means to buy in as a team-mate.

And the boards have begun to affirm and support these free-wheeling ministries which got their start on the edge of organized church life—without crimping anyone's style! The diaconate decided to send Kenney Sieck, our Firehouse director, to The Church of The Saviour and The Potter's House in Washington, D.C., for a week of training and growth. Listening carefully to what he has to say—in his fresh, unvarnished way—they are convinced that God has a great plan for his life. And they are creating a special Firehouse committee to encourage and help in that whole ministry.

The church council has put The Glory House into our budget, believing that this is a part of our mission. And Byron and the board of Christian education are offering to give a lift to the content and direction of small group life for those who want it, encouraging more people to give these groups a try, seeing them as a powerful part of our whole adult teaching ministry. And all this is only a foretaste of more to come.

Now don't let me mislead you. We still have some awfully up-tight, unimaginative church meetings, where we waste all kinds of precious time haggling over little stuff as though it really mattered. And every now and then someone's ugly feelings or an immature spirit of competition can wreck a meeting. Thank God we can go home and clean out before we come back to give it another try.

But far more important than this old resistance has been the new life seeping into our sacred institutional closets.

Even among our staff. There is no place where snarled feelings and unholy competition can raise its ugly head in more devious ways than among some custodians, pastors, musicians, and secretaries gathered to promote a "religious program for the congregation"! Yet, even here something is happening. Our last staff retreat at the Maury Paulsens' ended with a communion service that really was a time of affirmation and thanks.

Of course, we've had staff meetings of one kind or another for years. Talking over the church calendar, checking on the use of rooms or equipment, even venting some of our questions and irritations now and then and then trying to have some kind of prayer or devotional thought, which has usually been a rather proper sort of surface exercise.

When we've tried to move into deeper waters there has been a hidden resistance, a holding back, which neither my persuasiveness nor my position as senior pastor could overcome. Perhaps that's been the trouble. But more and more some of us have wondered, "Isn't there something better than this?"

Then our organist and senior staff member, Maynard Berk, came home from a two-month sabbatical in Europe with a new light in his eyes. Not just because of all the music that had flooded his life in one cathedral and concert hall after another—Cologne, Notre Dame, Ste. Clothilde, St. Peter's, Mechelen, and the other places. But more because he had been asked to join a Christian communal group in Utrecht for Bible study. Ichthus, they called themselves, meaning "the fish." It was, as Maynard reported, a taste of New Testament life, sweeping away all language and cultural barriers. And he seemed eager for more of the same.

About this time Howard Nelson, our warm-hearted chief custodian, came bouncing into our staff coffee one Saturday like a carefree child, just home from the University of Minnesota Medical Center. He had gone up there expecting to have open heart surgery. Of course we had gathered in prayer for him. And now here he was. At the end of a week of all kinds of tests the verdict had been "no surgery." He turned out to be one of those peculiar people with a double aorta. All Howard could say was, "Well, our prayers have been answered." And his joy spilled over all of us. I saw him then with new eyes and realized how much he had been giving the rest of us—preachers and all.

So we came to Maury and Carolyn Paulsens' home for a staff retreat. It was a lovely day full of surprises—with much thanks and affirmation. The communion service at the end was an invitation to a deeper life together.

At our regular staff meeting the following Monday we launched into the Epistle to the Ephesians, which has so much to say to us about the church. And at times over the next weeks there were flashes of something real, but most of the time it was a rather stiff, self-conscious effort. We couldn't quite seem to let go. Finally we finished the epistle three months or so later. And I was a bit surprised that the rest of them wanted to give the gospel of Matthew a try.

It was when we got to Jesus' great sermon that something began to open up. We couldn't deal with those simple, clean words without being touched where we really lived. "How blest are those who know their need of God; the kingdom of Heaven is theirs." [3] "If someone slaps you on the right cheek, turn and offer him your left." [4] That was the day one of our people got up and walked across the room and spoke some tender, halting words to another in the circle. We could only sit silently for a moment or two, giving thanks.

And then we got to that section where Jesus deals so directly with our nervous lack of trust. "Therefore I bid you put away anxious thoughts about food and drink to keep you alive, and clothes to cover your body. . . . Look at the birds of the air; they do not sow and reap and store in barns, yet your heavenly Father feeds them." [5] It was then that Victor Balla, our associate pastor and my loving teammate, spoke with some pain about his need for forgiveness. "Not just now and then but every day in large doses." Who would have thought it? Victor, who has been teaching us to sing with that beautiful, gregarious sense of Hungarian humor. But there it was.

Like a cry—spoken for all of us.

Well, it seems that after all these years something is happening. Shaking us up and freeing us. A church staff is actually becoming a trusting, open family. Which means we can even deal with our hidden agenda—the snarls in the record system that keep us apart, those little empires we can build that shut people out, the frustration over answering the phone—all that kind of thing. But now a new chapter in our ministry to the congregation has begun.

There is also a spirit of hospitality coming among our people. We catch some of this in our "house parties"—casual coffee-drinking affairs for new friends and seekers who want to meet one another and some of the church crowd. There's so much fun and laughter at these get-togethers it's a little hard to realize they can be sponsored by the deacons and deaconesses.

We ask folks with a gift for entertaining to open their home to any who may choose to come—usually twenty to thirty. There's a knack about doing this right. Is there anything more deadly than one of those church affairs where people end up in a big circle looking at one another trying to balance a cup and think of something to say?

So why not let some of these suburban people, who know all about the afternoon of bridge or the neighborhood coffee or the cocktail hour, give a low-key party for Jesus, now that they've met him. Most of them do it gladly! And really make people feel at ease. Don't you suppose it was a little like this when Zacchaeus or Matthew had Jesus home for dinner?

People are eager to let us know about their children—and more so their grandchildren. Ask me. I've become a grandfather since I started writing this book. And they usually are happy to tell how they met "on a blind date" or at our "dearest friend's wedding." It's amazing what comes out when we ask them to answer a simple question like "What person has most deeply influenced your life?" or "Have you had some lifting, positive experience in the past few weeks that you can share with the group?" These are usually warm, human times when people get a little taste of what it's all about.

Then someone will speak a word for Christ, naturally and simply. "He has really changed everything. You ought to see the way things are at home now. And the guys at work can hardly understand what's going on." Then there may be some honest, searching questions thrown out which the lay people handle beautifully. Then a time of joining hands and prayer before we take off for home, grateful and rejoicing. Most of the people who buy in with us come by this route.

But there's also been all kinds of informal, unstructured hospitality, which is probably the best kind. Like Harry and Addie Graber, who decided after a family council to have Eddie O'Shoniyi, a student from Africa, spend Christmas with them. But they really wondered if they could do this. Now that they were semi-retired why should they break up their orderly routine by taking in a stranger, especially at Christmas? But they did—and had the time of their lives! They still talk about it.

Think of what we would have missed if our people hadn't opened their homes to fatigued pastors, Faith at Work friends, teenagers passing through, and all kinds of visiting "firemen." Coffee and meals and beds—but really the lives of our people—have been shared from Hilltop to Riverview Heights. Sometimes with sleeping bags all over the place! Just imagine what we've been given.

But the "strangers," the hurting ones, have also come our way, looking for a "place," some sanctuary of healing and acceptance. Word gets around if the door is really open.

Jean was one of the first ones. She came from the West Coast to have her baby. Her pastor had called for help. Well, where could we "put her up"? First thing we tried the Schrags, whose eleven-year-old son Forry had died suddenly with a peculiar brain disease a few months earlier. And after a family huddle they agreed to give it a try. So Jean came on the bus all the way from San Jose, with her defenses a mile high. But little by little Kathy brought Jean into their family circle with a kind of loving firmness she needed. Not just by joining hands at meals to pray, but by getting her to handle some of the basics—making her bed and helping with the dishes. And Jean began to relax and join the human race.

One day I came on Jean so excited and breathless in the Park Ridge Shopping Center she almost knocked me down. "Look at this beautiful maternity dress!" she shouted. "And guess who bought it for me? Kathy!"

No one in the congregation, as far as I know, ever raised an eyebrow or breathed a derogatory remark as Jean became more obviously pregnant. And after the baby had come and Lutheran Social Services had placed it in a strong home, Jean went home with a new light in her eye. Of course, there had been problems and tensions during her stay. Jean was a disorganized, careless kind of human being. But she left more with us than she took.

That was a foretaste of things to come. I'm not certain how many girls have come our way through one arrangement or another, "carrying babies," troubled and guilt-ridden, seeking some way out of their dilemma. And beautiful, understanding people in our congregation—Dave and Fran Stewart, Merle and Sharon Johnson, Wes and Gail Nelson, Maury and Carolyn Paulsen, Jan Pay—and others like them, have taken them in.

And then there were John and Eleanor Erickson who welcomed Renetta Engles for a week or so, until we could find something more permanent. Renetta had come to us through an amazing series of circumstances. A dear Faith at Work friend, Heidi Frost, had heard sobbing through the wall in a motel in El Dorado, Kansas. When she could no longer stand it, she went next door and found Renetta, a heap of misery, longing for friendship and help. She had been through a legalized abortion and extensive mental treatment after three or four attempts at suicide. "I know just the place for you," Heidi told her. "I have a friend in Sioux Falls." Then she called us and said Renetta was on her way "if we'd have her." In a few hours we were picking Renetta up at the airport. It turned out I had baptized her when she was eleven years old in that first pastorate in Ottawa.

Well, after Renetta had been with the Ericksons a few days they simply wouldn't let her go. "She's got to stay with us," they insisted, "and that includes the girls." So the few days became a year . . . and Renetta left a different person to begin a life of her own. Talk about tough love!

But I guess it was Flo Reddicks who helped us see what was really taking place among us. Flo was a lovely black girl from Frogmore, South Carolina—she certainly took some razzing about that name—who had come to live with us while she finished her college work. No strings, only that she become a part of our family. Miriam had just taken off for college and the house had become awfully quiet without any of her impromptu singing at the piano or her giggling girl friends dropping in at all hours or those constant arrangements she kept making by telephone.

But Flo helped us with all that. She brought her own kind of

Here's where we do our business, in a beautiful colonial style structure that stands out over the neighborhood like a graceful watchman.

The conviction that life can break forth in the middle of the establishment has kept me working with this one congregation now for fifteen years.

God is
allowing me
to be part
of all that he
is doing
to this
congregation.

Renetta Engles
came to stay
for a week or so—
and left after a year,
a different person,
to begin a life
of her own.

Wes Nelson and I
met in a time of
beautiful
reconciliation.

Flo Reddicks brought
her own kind of excitement,
mainly her two-year-old
daughter
Antia—
a beautiful child,
as well as a mimic
and a saucy little lady.

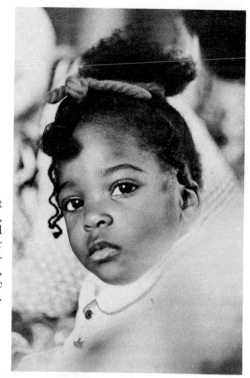

Evans Nord
is becoming
deeply
concerned about
how the life of
Christ can come
through in
Channel 11
in an honest,
natural way.

excitement, mainly her two-year-old daughter Antia—a beautiful child, as well as a mimic and a saucy little lady, who simply captivated the heart of our neighborhood. And incidentally did more for race relations than a dozen well-intentioned resolutions.

Ruth and I had a marvelous time with these two, and our son Joel and Flo became deep, lifelong friends.

The surprise came one day when Flo asked about joining our church. After all, we are basically a lily white, middle-class congregation. Ardie and Lenora Hayes are the only black people in our membership. So I clumsily tried to explain she was under no obligation, that staying with us was not a "rice Christianity" proposition. "Oh, I know that," she said. "I wouldn't be interested at all if it were. I want to join because there's all kinds of love there! I can feel it!" And it was quite a day when she came walking forward—stately and unhurried—giving herself to our people.

"All kinds of love there." That was *the* gift—more than any other. It meant we are becoming a Body—a living, growing organism. And that is a miracle that could happen only if the Holy Spirit is among us! A very real and specific happening, yet a mystery that goes beyond our capacity to explain. In spite of our mistakes and unbelief, Christ has been accepting whatever obedience and trust we have been giving him, drawing us together.

We can sense this in the way people greet one another when they gather for worship and so often linger afterwards, not wanting to leave! This is particularly true of our "People's Service" Sunday evenings. Folks coming together in little knots here and there—talking, laughing, and often praying softly.

Or you can get the feel of this seeing Willett Gibbs being helped down the aisle for Sunday morning worship at 8:30. Here comes this simple, childlike man—ninety-three years of age—hobbling in again to join "his" family. Often it is Jay Parker, an eager college student, or Mel Forseth, a heating and air-conditioning contractor, or Loren Crary, our city electrical inspector, making sure he gets to his pew. A small, quiet demonstration of what it means to bear one another's burdens.

If the life of this Body is authentic, people will always be loved and affirmed. This is the constant work of the Spirit. And in this context they can discover their gifts and enter the ministry into which Christ is calling them. More and more we see that happening. This is a far different matter than doing busy institutional church work out of a sense of guilt or duty.

So every service of worship or teaching experience becomes a setting, a womb, in which this "calling forth of gifts" can take place. The same is true of every board or committee meeting. Often, pushing or leading people out into deep water, laying on them some special burden in the name of Christ, can become their moment of discovery and awakening.

Much of our training has been "on the job"—in a board meeting or on a call. Don't you suppose this is the way Jesus dealt with the twelve, or Barnabas encouraged Saul on that first missionary journey, and in turn Paul brought Timothy and Luke and Silas and so many others into the ministry of Christ? Not in some vague, theoretical way, but in the heat and nitty-gritty of concrete life situations. Even prison.

Often one of us on the pastoral staff will take a lay person—one of the people of God—along on a call, evangelistic or pastoral. Or into a place of crisis or need. A visit to the state mental hospital at Yankton or to the state penitentiary on the hill or to a home where death has come or into a courtroom for a special hearing. This has often been a moment of teaching, a time when gifts of compassion and insight and witness can begin to stir.

Little by little we are seeing a powerful pastoral ministry emerge among our people. No question that people like Jerry Adrian or Bill Flaskey or Dorothy Ruyter or Marlene Palmer, and others like them, have a beautiful, growing ministry with people.

So Mary Thome was willing, in spite of her holding back at first, to give the care of our sick and shut-in members a try. And it was almost as if her forty-four years with the State Department of Education had been preparing her for this. Her sensitivity and compassion and a remarkable gift for administration simply blossomed. She ended up coordinating all our lay pastoral care for these people, enlisting strong help like Florence Parker, the head housekeeper at Sioux Valley Hospital, and a host of others.

Or why should Ila Million sit alone in retirement after serving Sioux Falls College as Assistant Registrar for fourteen years? She has become almost a full-time secretary, answering the phone during staff meetings and keeping all the assignments of the diaconate in order.

We could not carry on the affairs of the church without a host of volunteers who have joined us in the mission: those who are now answering the church telephone or helping with special projects in the building; Joyce Blount and Marilyn Woodden making the kitchen a special place of ministry; Pat Peterson taking the rosebuds and a word of love out to the new mothers; Inga Paulson spending hours on the phone setting up appointments for our church callers; Mable Eggland coming in after work to keep our membership records in order. The list goes on and on—a rich diversity of gifts becoming a beautiful harmony to the glory of God!

But it isn't just the "in church" business. There are the gifts that Christ shares with his people for ministry in the marketplace. The worship and life of the church must encourage and enable people to be his servants on Monday morning!

So when Lowell Hansen met Christ last year, the excitement hit his bus terminal, Jackrabbit Lines, on North Dakota Avenue. The men who drink coffee with him wondered, "What has happened to Lowell?" And he and Carol talked about giving a new kind of Christmas party for their friends.

Or Ron Sheard, who came alive on a lay witness team, and came home wanting to be baptized that very night. He keeps wondering how others can know Christ is alive because he's working at a cutting bench at Morrell's.

Or Evans Nord, manager and vice president of a TV station, becoming deeply concerned about how the life of Christ can come through on Channel 11 in an honest, natural way. At a recent Bible study group he put it beautifully. "When I got into this Christian thing again, I picked up this cross to carry in my pocket as a reminder. At first I tried to make certain the cross stayed in my pocket when I reached for change. But now I bring it right out with the loose change because there's nothing to hide. And people may even ask me about it. Which is great!"

The Spirit can gather all this up and make it the life of a people, sharing their gifts to the glory of God! I don't have to do it all—trying to prove I'm kind of a super-duper director carrying on a one-man show! No, I can be one of the encouragers, an equipper, so that the *laos*, the people of God, can find their ministry.

10.

So
Who's
a Loser?

This started out to be a human success story. That's the way I was putting it together, almost unconsciously. Everything would come out glossy and "Pepsodent clean" and freshly packaged. The hurt feelings and jagged edges and unfinished business would be covered up.

But then I heard a phrase at a Faith at Work meeting in Baltimore that really shook me up and set me to thinking. A young Presbyterian minister, Howard Childers, was telling us about the things going on in his church in Littleton, Colorado. I can still see him, all excited, standing behind the piano. All of a sudden his hands came down with a bang and he almost shouted, "Man, what we've got is a church for losers." That was the only note I scrawled, on a borrowed piece of paper, during our three days together—"a church for losers."

But that certainly wasn't our story—or was it? As I thought about that wonderful conglomeration of people back home I couldn't help wondering. Not just the ragged cripples. The obvious sinners. But the respectable, proper ones. All being drawn by our Lord to a common banquet table, coming only with his invitation in hand.

I could close my eyes and see them gathering for worship— coming to celebrate the mystery of God's forgiveness once again.

Gene Koch, who was so new with us. Sitting about a third of the way back on the center aisle in the eleven o'clock service. A huge bear of a man with a mustache and shaggy black hair. With a quiet, joyful glow about him now, like a fire, but carrying the marks of the old life in drugs on his arms. Gene had called one day because he had met Christ, wanting to know if there were someone he could talk with. So Victor put him in touch with Kenney Sieck, who took him in tow. And they became inseparable friends—missionaries at The Firehouse.

Or Tom Harkison, sitting with his family halfway back on the south side. Staying close to the window so he could see a little, and greet some of his old familiar friends—one of our stalwart, pioneering spirits. A retired banker, now a financial advisor to many of the town greats, and a driving force in urban renewal. Simply grateful to be here once more after all his difficulties with his health—a forgiven sinner like the rest of us. Greatly concerned about the whole ministry of the church.

Or Bev Weiss, quite often right up in the front pew with the prayer group. She had called for help at the bottom of the pit of alcoholism. And Christ waited for her at the end of all those blackouts and fear. It was a complete, unequivocal act of surrender, or she never would have made it. Now she was a deaconess radiating a serenity that was a blessing to the rest of us.

And right next to her Martha Carlson or Ila Million, beautiful, straight Christians who had never known anything like Bev's experience. But rejoicing in their life of forgiveness too! And that's why they had been set free to minister in the name of Christ.

That's the way it ran all the way from the front pew to the balcony—at any one of our services. An amazing mixture gathered by the grace of God, seeking, struggling, celebrating, and learning. God's people. Maybe we were a church for losers after all.

Then my mind moved to a Sunday evening when Randy Lawson had come forward in our People's Service. A free spirit, one of the bearded "Jesus people" at the college—"Wolfman" the students called him—coming to "buy in" with an institutional church. He was greeted by all the young people on hand with an almost ecstatic joy. I was a bit surprised when I saw Hilda Hendricksen and Elda Stevens struggling to get through all that exuberance. As one of them said, "We just have to meet that young man." How marvelous, I thought, that these two steady, matronly Christians would be coming to greet someone from this other world. But then

I wondered, is there any "other world"? Isn't there only one family? Of course! That's why Hilda and Elda were coming to be Randy's "shepherds."

Well, by now this "loser" business was so deep in me I had to share it with our people. So the following Sunday I brought that borrowed scrap of paper with that scrawl on it into the pulpit and asked the congregation if that wasn't really who we were. "Losers?" After all, look at how we had come—with fears, insecurities, and guilt so much a part of our existence. And houses and money and education didn't make much difference because we were really all in the same boat.

But weren't we "losers" who had found a new beginning in Christ? And that's why we had become a people of hope. Our worst enemies—mainly death and guilt—had been defeated. Christ had taken care of all that at the cross and in the power of his resurrection. So we were no longer "under condemnation"!

I was amazed how much of the Bible zeros in on this "loser" theme. Jesus insisted that none of us will ever make it unless we get off our high horse! "How blest are those who know their need of God. . . . How blest are the sorrowful. . . . How blest are those of a gentle spirit." [1] There is no other way. And he keeps encouraging us to really trust his Father. "No, do not ask anxiously, 'What are we to eat? What are we to drink? What shall we wear?' All these are things for the heathen to run after, not for you, because your heavenly Father knows that you need them all." [2]

There's not much pompous talk when he sends out the seventy. "Look, I am sending you like lambs among wolves." [3]

Paul, who is so often like a flaming, passionate lion, also talks like a scared little boy when he writes to the Corinthians. "I came before you weak, nervous, and shaking with fear." [4] But later on he says he had discovered God's answer—" 'My grace is all you need; power comes to its full strength in weakness.' " [5] That's the great surprise in all this—God's strength in our weakness. Well, all of this got into the sermon. At the end I simply asked, "Then who are we?"

The response was almost overwhelming. People had really listened and heard, and felt affirmed. They said things like, "Man, you were really with it today." "Thanks for being so honest." "Is it ever a relief that I don't have to prove anything."

Two weeks later this was all confirmed, openly. As we were singing our last hymn in the eleven o'clock service there was a stirring in the balcony. And here came Rich and Priscilla Gorsuch with their sons Eric and Zane—nervous, but all excited, and eager to confess Christ.

I almost surprised myself by asking if they wanted to share a word with the congregation. But without any hesitation Rich responded, "We've come because we want to be a part of this family." With Priscilla, though, it was different. There was a long moment of waiting, and I was certain I had made a mistake. Then she said very quietly, "If this weren't a place for losers we wouldn't be here. But it is, and that's why we've come." There was a choked hush, then a prayer of thanks before the "losers" started greeting and affirming one another. What a celebration that turned out to be!

I had met the Gorsuches at a wedding dinner a couple of years before, and had learned about Rich's encounter with Christ at the Mayo Clinic. After days of testing for some back trouble, one of the physicians had almost inadvertently discovered a misty blur behind the heart on the X-ray. It turned out to be a huge cyst, attached to the esophagus, pressing into his heart. So the doctors decided on immediate chest surgery. Everything now had become a matter of life and death for Rich.

In the long night between diagnosis and surgery Rich had to ask all those big questions he had been running from all his life. "What is the meaning of it all?" "If I don't make it, what then?" "I wonder what it would be like to really know God?" "Do I dare trust my future to him?"

So in a kind of blind helplessness Rich cried out for help. It was an act of surrender. And God heard, even though it was months before Rich understood what had happened. But he went into surgery with an unexplainable peace, even a joyful abandon, flooding his life.

Rich desperately needed that peace. He had been out to make it big in a hurry in the ad agency business. Self-centered and aggressive, but full of confusion and conflict. Too much booze and a mass of tangled relationships had almost finished his marriage —and his business. And all the time he was prostituting a sensitive artistic ability.

All this came out in a short, gritty visit at that wedding dinner.

It was the beginning of a trusting, deepening friendship.

Not long after that first encounter I stopped by to look in on a showing of original paintings Rich was having at Home Federal Savings and Loan. Lovely, haunting expressions. Once you had seen them, you couldn't forget them. As I casually moved around I couldn't help noticing that in every painting something was alone—a pump or a tree or a house—almost forlorn. It was as if Rich were saying, "Here I am, all empty and alone. Will someone help me find my place? I want to belong."

It was then I scrawled a note of thanks and slipped it by Rich's agency with a copy of Keith Miller's *The Taste of New Wine*,[6] which I took along almost as an afterthought. Rich was there. Later on he reminded me that I stood in his office and really laid it on him. "You don't want to stay here. You really want to leave this place and go with Christ. All the way." A couple of days later I found a note on my desk—in a scrawl that was barely legible. "Thanks. Reading *The Taste of New Wine* was like reading my own subconscious. Rich."

One thing led to another. In December he ended up joining Bob Olson and me on a month-long tour of our mission stations in Southeast Asia. He was simply longing to get near as much of this living stuff as he could right at the start. The three of us got almost more than we could handle. Moving from Tokyo to Iloilo City in the Philippines, from Hong Kong to Saigon, and from Calcutta and Jorhat to Rangoon, we met and lived with a handful of God's courageous, eager people at every place we put down. People who were pouring out their lives with a reckless abandon, surrounded by masses whose never-ending needs were simply staggering! Bob, who had a special love for children, kept saying, "Look at all those kids." It was an awesome and emotionally draining experience, yet far more a journey into hope, than into despair. And every time we got on a plane it seemed Rich would open his paperback *New English Bible* and begin asking questions, searching, trying to put it all together.

It was in Hopevale in the Philippines that the real crunch came—back in the hill country of Panay. A special holy place of martyrdom where eleven of our Baptist missionaries had been massacred by the Japanese one Sunday morning early in the Second World War. Here at a place called the Cathedral in the Glen, the great pastor of the hills, Dianala, seventy-one years of age, lean and tough, the man whose congregation had sustained this little band for twenty-two months before death came, led us in reading the Beatitudes. Who of us will ever forget those simple, powerful "blesseds"? Then he asked for prayer. And when a young Japanese student began to pray in his own language, there was a sob. It was the first time the Japanese tongue had been heard in that place since the awful days of the war. All Dianala could do was go over and embrace him— a beautiful act of healing. There was no possibility of our leaving untouched. As we worked our way back through the jungle, Rich could only say, "I'll never be the same."

No sooner had we gotten home than he began to make good on that vow. First it was a time of retreat and painting with a passionate urgency. "Sentinels of Hope" he called them. A girl in Hong Kong with a brother on her back—an old man on the streets of Calcutta—a one-legged Vietnamese veteran on the steps of a hospital in Saigon—two of those powerful Philippine hill people from Dianala's congregation—sensitive, arresting stuff—six faces of Asia on canvas. Five of them are now hanging in our church.

Next it was a drastic change in his calling. Less and less the big deal operator and more and more the sensitive Christian communicator, struggling and innovating to make Christ real in the marketplace. Affirming and asking in a hundred ways, "I love you. Is that OK?"

Then it was the family. Always the toughest because here nothing can be swept under the rug. How do you straighten things out there when you've lived in competition and disorder for years? No way unless Christ really gets a chance.

At first, all of Rich's spiritual pushing and effervescing only drove Priscilla further away, angry and defensive. Why not? After all, she had weathered at least a dozen of his jags before. So if she left him alone maybe this latest one would pass too. But it didn't! In fact she began to sense a new tenderness and patience in Rich, and even a struggle to be honest. There seemed to be something different this time.

She couldn't help wondering. After all, she was sick unto death of playing her own games. The proper, uptight Priscilla who kept cleaning the house over and over again, trying so desperately to keep everything under control, while that other self, the ugly demonic one, kept breaking through. No way she could talk this away or push it down. So here she was, torn between entertaining the ladies' aid circle early in the evening and hurrying off into the night for another kind of encounter.

Finally that desperate conflict brought her to the end—with five weeks on the psych ward at McKennan followed by months of therapy. And even after all that, she was driven back to her lost and lonely merry-go-round of horror. But always there was the deeper cry, "With my whole being I thirst for you, the living God." [7]

It was at the bottom of all this that Rich brought Priscilla to my office. All I could do was hold this trembling, disheveled woman close for some moments and assure her that I was not afraid of her, and that there was hope, spelled capital H O P E, because Jesus Christ loved her, just like she was, and he could change her. That day Priscilla quietly took a drink of Living Water, and her thirst was quenched—at the end of all that frantic running. A miracle, just as it was for another woman at a well, centuries ago.

And she too hurried home to tell the others—Rich and her sons —that she had met One who had begun to satisfy her deepest longing. That was the beginning of a gentle healing in the Gorsuch home that is still going on. The home has become more and more a stopping off place, a shelter, for all kinds of people, mostly the long-haired, the confused and the seekers.

That's why the Gorsuches got up that day in the balcony to join the rest of us—Gene Koch, Tom Harkison, Bev Weiss, Martha Carlson, and all the others—losers every one of us.

But what does that mean—"losers every one of us"? That we're a bunch of cripples, always wanting someone's sympathy, whiners who never succeed at anything, perpetual confessers sitting around pawing over our old sins? Is that what this is? Well, I hope not, because if it is, then I want out fast.

But if it's a company of people who can be real and open with one another, knowing they are sinners constantly needing the grace of God—people who can say to one another, "I need you," or "Will you forgive me?" because they have first been forgiven— people who have been set free to laugh and cry with one another without being ashamed—then this will be a family of healing and newness. And ordinary people will begin doing extraordinary things because the Spirit is among them. If that's what a church for losers is all about, then I want in. For keeps!

We have been discovering these realities together. Like in a recent church council meeting when Tom Idema abruptly blurted out, "Rich, you scare the hell out of me. You are so free I freeze up inside every time I get around you. That's why I often try to avoid you." Then we watched Rich turn to Tom in amazement. "Man, if you only knew how scared I am inside. Why I'm a little lonely boy much of the time." And all of us sat there for a heavy moment before these two men reached out and grabbed one another.

Which liberated LeRoy Day so he could confess that he hadn't wanted to come, not only because he didn't have his homework done or had a hundred things to do at the college, but because he wasn't quite sure how deeply he wanted to buy in with this council or how far he could trust us. And right then and there he was given a joyous affirmation by the group.

No wonder the whole meeting became a hilarious celebration full of prayer and healing. This is "being church to one another," as Byron puts it. We're learning about that.

Out of that single meeting just a few months ago, some creative, beautiful things have already been let loose that are beginning to shape the life of our congregation. But had we sat there isolated and cut off from one another, each with his own hidden agenda, without anyone making a move, then it would have been another sterile, proper church meeting with nothing happening. It took that first move to open the rest of us.

Would you believe that while these very words are being written, Margie Scott called all breathless and concerned. She was to have a devotional for a women's group this afternoon and didn't want to goof it. So she called for a bit of encouragement. And in the midst of the conversation said, "By the way, have you read 'I Watched Rosanna Die' by Philip Hoh in *The American Baptist?* Because that's my story. If I hadn't gone through the long, painful struggle to find myself—and I wanted to die a hundred times—I never could have come alive."

That's right. But people affirmed and supported Margie, especially the Wendell Cooks, when she wasn't too pleasant to be around, whining and unhappy, during her death.

But then the Resurrection came. In a lot of ways. Some of it through that Sunday night "gift" group. Here she was affirmed and discovered she had something to share. So one evening in a People's Service, Margie stood up and asked if she might not sing something she had written. It was a simple, plaintive song about God's love—a gift to all of us. Somehow we knew that night that Margie was going to be all right. Then we discovered she was sewing all kinds of lovely things for people, doing some painting, baking bread and rolls out of her meager resources, giving them to the people she loved.

Who would have thought all this was locked up in Margie until the heartache and suffering had broken her open and released it? Like the perfume another woman broke out and poured on the feet of Jesus. This is what a church for losers is all about.

But in the end it was me! I had to learn the whole loser style for myself. Not theoretically, nor as a technique for operating a church, but as a way of life right in the heat of battle—meeting those incessant preaching deadlines, trying to bring angry husbands and wives together, constantly trying to bring some order into each day's tangled pressures, trying to stay with people long enough, the hurting, bleeding ones as well as those apparently self-sufficient ones, so we could share our lives with one another in some kind of helpful way. That's where I learned some of this.

I have discovered over and over again how inadequate and needy I really am, and have been thrown back on the sufficiency of God and the acceptance of his people so that I might "fully grow up into Christ" [8] with them. It's been a painful, humiliating experience, because on the surface I come through so often as being on top of things, able to charm people into getting things done. Affable, friendly, and gregarious—but needing to be liked and approved at times almost to a fault. And underneath often a scared little boy trying to prove that everything is all right. So these people, who have known me and yet have let me be myself, even letting me fail but still loving me, have been God's special gift.

But it's been at home where I've learned this the best—with that intimate, tender, but honest circle of people who really know me. Who have put up with my constant flood of new ideas, my latest projects, my absent-minded, scattered ways, and my drive to save the world one way or another. And yet have loved me! That's where my deepest freedom has come.

It has been
Ruth who
has understood
and shared
her life with me
most fully—
a sweetheart,
helpmate
and friend.

Margie Scott sews
all kinds of lovely things,
doing some painting,
baking bread and rolls
out of her meager resources,
giving them to the people she loves.

In the end it
was me!
I had to learn
the whole loser
style for
myself.

Randy, our oldest, is now in Rapid City as an aide to U.S. Senator James Abourezk, finding his own ministry among all those needing the special resources of the government—the elderly who simply cannot make it on the Social Security check, the servicemen from nearby Ellsworth Air Force Base facing crisis situations, and the Indians coming day after day desperately seeking for justice. Quite an assignment.

In earlier years Randy and I were often more than subtly competitive. But now we have become the dearest of friends as father and son. He often calls me "brother" or "Roger," which I gratefully accept as an affirmation. We have always had a special love for the water and some years ago even built a Sailfish together which our son Joel promptly dubbed "The Noskirderf," spelling Fredrikson backwards.

So it was a special delight to receive a sailing mobil from Randy at Christmas a couple of years ago, and with it his unique greeting: "For: The High Priest of Melchizidek [that's an in joke] . . . a little reminder that (& hope that) we five *Noskirderfs* are mates forever! From: Your (sometimes) prodigal (but always hopeful) Son."

Then there is Miriam, married to Frank Lemp, who is now finishing his first challenging year of teaching art to junior highers in Leavenworth, Kansas, and coaching wrestling. Miriam is the beautiful mother of our first grandchild Elizabeth, called Liserl because of Frank's Austrian background. Miriam and I have had some real donnybrooks over the years because we are both strong-willed and hot-tempered. But always with some kind of a reconciliation at the end.

And throughout the struggle of this writing Miriam has kept the encouragement coming my way. "Good luck on the book, Dad" or "We're praying you're going to get it done."

Well, some years ago, when Miriam was finally elected cheerleader in her senior year at Washington High School after two earlier unsuccessful attempts, she left a note with a candy sucker glued to it on my desk. She knew I was really pulling for her. "Thanks for your encouragement, Dad. Your cheerleading daughter." I found it when I dropped by the office late one afternoon. It was her unique way of letting me know she'd made it. And I was filled with a warm glow, grateful that encouragement is a two-way street.

Then there is Joel, now a college senior and into music back at the old stomping grounds at Ottawa—with long hair down to his shoulders. More gentle and introspective than the others. He came home during spring break a year ago and quietly announced that at the end of a long confusing search, with some drugs thrown in, he had been baptized in the Holy Spirit, and that now his life had been filled with praise and wonder. We could only sit at the supper table, silently and gratefully, thanking God for his goodness.

Joel had completely devastated me once before at a communion service when he was serving as a deacon. He was then a senior in high school. We had encouraged all our people to step out and greet one another in the name of Christ before eating and drinking the Supper. I was about to step back to Lester McGee, who was in church for the first time since taking Burton, his wife of more than fifty years, to Luther Manor. She had become more and more senile and it was the only thing he could do. And here he was with all that suffering etched in his face.

But just as I moved from behind the communion table, Joel caught me by the arm and spoke ever so softly, "In the name of Christ, Dad, I love you." I was so overwhelmed I could hardly get through the service.

So it has gone through the years. An unexpected word or touch coming just at the right time from these closest to me.

But it has been Ruth who has understood and shared her life with me most fully. Gracious, unselfish, and patient—a sweetheart, helpmate and friend! I wonder how many times she has waited for me—after church, at mealtime, at some airport, or late at night. Never holding back her quiet trust or stubborn honesty. Two or three times I'm certain I would have moved on—with the mission unfinished—had it not been for her steadying influence. How often she has kept me on target simply asking, "Are you sure?"

I have never left for another one of our heavy Sundays after an early breakfast, usually walking down to church, without her saying "Power to you!" She has understood and loved my mother, a woman of great strength and courage, now in her seventy-ninth year, who would have gone under long ago, particularly after my father and brother died, had it not been for her faith!

But all this can become familiar, be the expected thing, and even be taken for granted, until circumstances draw us up short and force us to see those we love with new eyes. It was that way when asthma came to Ruth, treacherously and unexpectedly, after thirty-five years of good health. It started with a bronchial infection and within hours she was fighting for every breath. In the next few hours I was to learn about adrenalin shots, i.v. feedings, respirators, and all the rest in a frighteningly first-hand way. And much more over the next five years during a dozen or so visits to the hospital. Twice there was sinus surgery and once a cardiac arrest. It's not necessary to go into any more of the ugly details.

A couple of times during all this our close friend and family physician, Bob Olson, sat with me outside our house after one of her attacks—I remember those visits well—and gave it to me straight. Ruth really needed me, not in snatches, but in whole chunks. All of me, as she had given herself to me so fully for years.

But even after that, whenever she became ill, I could always leave her with friendly understanding people—the nurses and aides and all the rest in Sioux Valley Hospital. After all, we know so many of them.

Until we found ourselves in a small community hospital in Ripon, Wisconsin. We had gone to the American Baptist Assembly near there for a laymen's conference where I was supposed to be one of the leaders. The air was heavy, and we had pushed ourselves to ferry across Lake Michigan to visit our dear friends, the Blair Helmans. As we were returning, the old tightening and the awful struggle for air started for Ruth. Then we were rushing off to find the hospital in Ripon.

It turned out to be a long, frightening attack. And this time there were none of the familiar faces around the hospital, although all kinds of beautiful, supportive friends began to show up unexpectedly. Especially Harold and Helen Larson, beloved friends from home who were there for the conference. And there was an unforgettable communion service in Ruth's room which Maurice Jackson brought to us.

But the routine was all strange, and this time I had nowhere to run. So I was forced to stay by and take a long, hard look at things. There was the day I went to the nurses' station to use the phone and inadvertently happened to see the doctor's scrawl on his pad. The words stood out like fire. "The apprehension of the patient's husband is not helping this case." I stood there stunned. Me? Why, wasn't I the cool, strong one when things like this came along? But that isn't what this doctor saw at all.

I dropped the phone and walked back to Room 207 into a long heavy night. A mixture of shame and wondering, of fear and prayer came over me, against the background of Ruth's heavy, hoarse gasping for breath. What had I really been doing all these years? How much had I missed knowing Ruth's needs? What was God trying to say to me?

In the midst of that night some kind of a light broke in. Not much, but a little. That I had always shunned sick women—one way or another—and Ruth had been no different. Something deep in me had turned away from her when she most needed me. So I would become very busy and actually avoid her. It was a painful, humiliating discovery, but the beginning of something new—a cleansing, a healing, a release which set me free to affirm Ruth with tears even though she was not consciously aware of what was going on.

Nothing dramatic or sudden happened then. In a few days, of course, we were on our way home. But something quiet and powerful began to unfold. A new tenderness and vulnerability between the two of us and with others.

That was three years ago. And Ruth has never returned to the hospital. It was the beginning of a miracle that is still opening before us. Which has made me unashamed to say that I, too, am a loser. Of course, I often slip back into the old ways. But then I am reminded one way or another once again who I really am—how dependent I am on God. And then the glory floods my life once again and I am able to reach out to others. We are learning to sing together, hesitatingly but expectantly,

> Breathe on me, Breath of God;
> Fill me with life anew,
> That I may love what Thou dost love,
> And do what Thou wouldst do.
> —EDWIN HATCH

notes

Chapter 1   Standing on Tiptoe
1. Dorothy L. Sayers, *Creed or Chaos?* (New York: Harcourt, Brace, 1949), pp. 5–6.
2. Romans 5:6.
3. Acts 2:24.
4. Mark 10:23.
5. Philippians 4:19, 13, 7.

Chapter 2   Signs of His Presence
1. Elizabeth Burns, *The Late Liz* (New York: Meredith Press, 1957).
2. Romans 12:2 (Phillips).
3. Exodus 3:11.

Chapter 3   The Open Agenda
1. Matthew 16:18.
2. Matthew 25:40.
3. John 7:37–38.

Chapter 4   Well, Here I Am
1. Romans 16:5; 1 Corinthians 16:19; Colossians 4:15; Philemon 1:2.
2. 2 Corinthians 12:9.
3. Galatians 2:20.

Chapter 5   A Bunch of Dandelions
1. Romans 16:3–5; Colossians 4:15; Philemon 1:2.
2. John 15:13.

3. *Good News for Modern Man,* The New Testament in Today's English Version (New York: American Bible Society, 1966, 1971).

Chapter 6   No Loitering in the Halls
1. Zechariah 4:6 (rsv).
2. Acts 13:2–3.

Chapter 7   It Just Doesn't Make Sense
1. Lawrence Baulch, *Return to the World* (Valley Forge: Judson Press, 1968).
2. Bill Milliken and Char Meredith, *Tough Love* (Old Tappan, N.J.: Fleming H. Revell, 1968).
3. John 1:12.

Chapter 8   Getting Their Brains Out of Hock
1. Ephesians 2:19.
2. Matthew 6:13.
3. Baulch, *Return to the World.*
4. Romans 1:17.
5. Luke 4:18.

Chapter 9   Meanwhile, Back at 22nd and Covell
1. 1 Peter 2:9.
2. Philippians 1:6.
3. Matthew 5:3.
4. Matthew 5:39.
5. Matthew 6:25–26.

Chapter 10   So Who's a Loser?
1. Matthew 5:3–5.
2. Matthew 6:31–32.
3. Luke 10:4.
4. 1 Corinthians 2:4.
5. 2 Corinthians 12:9.
6. Keith Miller, *The Taste of New Wine* (Waco, Texas: Word Books, 1965).
7. Psalm 42:2.
8. Ephesians 4:15.